Selections from the

M. & M. KAROLIK

Collection

of

American Paintings

$\frac{1815}{1865}$

Museum of Fine Arts

Boston

Picture Book Series
Library of Congress Catalogue Card Number 75–39918
ISBN 0–87846–095–0
Typeset by The Stinehour Press, Lunenburg, Vermont
Printed by The Leether Press, Boston, Massachusetts
Designed by Carl F. Zahn

Cover: ANONYMOUS. *Calligraphic Eagle with Scroll and Quill Pen.*
Pen, gray, black, and brown inks. 19 ⅝ x 27 ¾ in. 60.1127

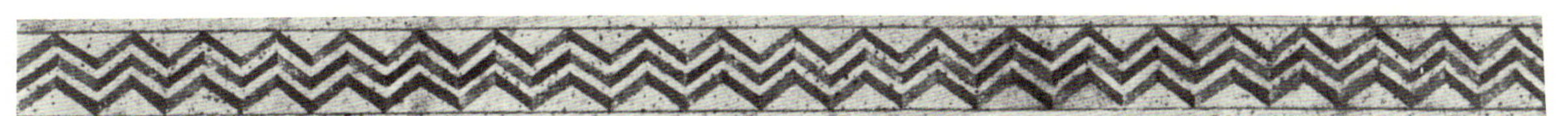

THREE of the most important and comprehensive collections of American art came to the Museum of Fine Arts between 1938 and 1962 as gifts of Maxim and Martha Karolik: the M. and M. Karolik Collection of 18th Century American Furniture, the M. and M. Karolik Collection of American Paintings, 1815–1865, and the M. and M. Karolik Collection of American Water Colors and Drawings, 1800–1875. Over a period of twenty-seven years, Karolik, a native of Russia, and his wife, the former Martha Codman of Newport, Rhode Island, had been enthusiastic pioneer collectors of American art, acquiring objects with the advice and collaboration of the Boston Museum, which they had designated as the permanent home for their collections.

The Karolik Collection of American Paintings consists of nearly four hundred portraits, still lifes, landscapes, and genre paintings that reflect the social and physical character of the new nation from the Republic through the Civil War. At the time the collection was offered to the Museum of Fine Arts in 1945, Karolik wrote to Mr. G. H. Edgell, director of the museum: "It [the collection] was made for one purpose only: To show what happened in this country in the art of painting in the period of half a century—from 1815 to 1865—and to show the beginning and the growth of American landscape and genre painting. The aim was to make a collection not of 'Americana' for the antiquarian, but of American art for the nation. . . . We all know that this collection does not represent a 'School.' Traces of many influences may be found in it. But it is not necessary to be an expert to see that the beauty of this collection springs from the roots of this nation; that it contains its own national characteristics; that it expresses its own idiom, which is definitely American. In that idiom, I believe, lies the reason for its universal appeal."

The paintings presented here, which were chosen as being most representative of and closely identified with the Karolik collection, illustrate the development and variety of both academic and folk art.

IN THE FIRST QUARTER of the nineteenth century the establishment of American academies of art made it possible for professional painters to exhibit and see the work of other artists without travel to Europe, although the desire for study abroad persisted, and immigrating painters continued to bring with them a European heritage. After the War of 1812, when ties with England were finally dissolved, American artists became concerned with themes of interest to their own countrymen. History and portraiture, traditionally considered the noblest subjects for painting, were adapted to reflect the new spirit of nationalism. Episodes of American political and historical importance and national heroes were depicted as well as ordinary citizens—merchants, ministers, mothers, and children (nos. 6, 2, 3). Landscape painting was given new emphasis. References to the American countryside, which had hitherto been generalized and somewhat romanticized, assumed considerable accuracy in works by artists of the Hudson River School of landscape painting such as Thomas Cole (no. 5). Artists became patriotically conscious of celebrating and describing their country and portrayed not only the land but its link with the sea and the development of trade and towns along the eastern seaboard and inland waterways (nos. 15, 16, 31). Toward midcentury topographical realism was combined with a lyric quality, as a new awareness of light and atmosphere permeated landscape painting (nos. 30, 43).

Domestic and rural activities were also scrutinized by painters such as Clonney and Inman (nos. 19, 26). European compositions are known to have been utilized in part (no. 8), but because the character of these activities was uniquely American, the paintings in general have a directness despite an occasional tendency to moralize. For its story-telling aspects, genre painting drew increasingly on American folklore and literature as sources of inspiration (no. 9).

The discovery and settlement of the West provided seemingly inexhaustible material for artists, who fed and influenced their countrymen's curiosity about the new territories. Seth Eastman and Albert Bierstadt were among those who accompanied exploratory expeditions, recording Indian life as well as the landscape (nos. 17, 46); others depicted the white man's migration westward (nos. 29, 40).

Artists performed a similar critical and documentary function in regard to the Civil War. Paintings that ranged in viewpoint from factual report to political satire represented battle scenes as well as the effects of the war upon civilian life. This turbulent period is not shown in the paintings illustrated here, although examples are to be found in the Karolik collection of paintings and in greater number in the collection of watercolors and drawings. This selection concentrates on the more serene aspects of nineteenth century America as does the Karolik painting collection itself, in which the sense of confidence and opportunity of the pre–Civil War era prevails.

The work of American folk artists is well represented in the Karolik collection. Most of these artists, now also referred to as limners, naïve, primitive, or provincial painters, were largely self-taught. They had little or no contact with the academic tradition, with the result that their art is virtually free of artistic convention. Although a number of these artists and their works have been identified, many still remain unknown. From their paintings and existing records, we know that they lived and worked mainly in the small towns and villages of New England and New York State. They were often skilled craftsmen with a trade such as house painting, sign painting, or carriage decoration, which required talent and training. Thus, the artisans who turned to painting pictures brought with them considerable experience and knowledge of the craft and its materials.

Before the invention of photography, it was only through the artist that images could be recorded and preserved. Despite long distances and difficult travel, there were many itinerant artists who managed to journey across entire states, painting as they went. They made countless portraits of people in neighboring towns and of those they encountered during their travels (nos. 4, 11, 45). They painted views of towns, farms, animals, ships, scenes of everyday life, and even religious and historical themes (13, 48). Some of their ideas were copied from prints that were readily available to them, and some were straight out of their imagination. The distinct individuality of these artists and the fact that few show another's influence in their painting would seem to indicate that they pursued independent paths. Although their styles differ, common to their work is a remarkable sense of design and color, a strong, linear composition and the direct, unselfconscious manner in which they tried to depict what they saw. Inaccuracies in perspective and drawing frequently appear in their paintings, but it is these very characteristics that contribute to the highly expressive aspect of their work.

Thus, the folk artists began a tradition that was carried westward with the moving frontier and continues today. Their painting bears little resemblance to the other trends with which it coexisted, and it is perhaps the only art that emerged from this country during the nineteenth century nearly untouched by European influence. Their art and the spirit with which it was conceived are undeniably American.

Lucretia H. Giese
Laura C. Luckey
Department of Paintings

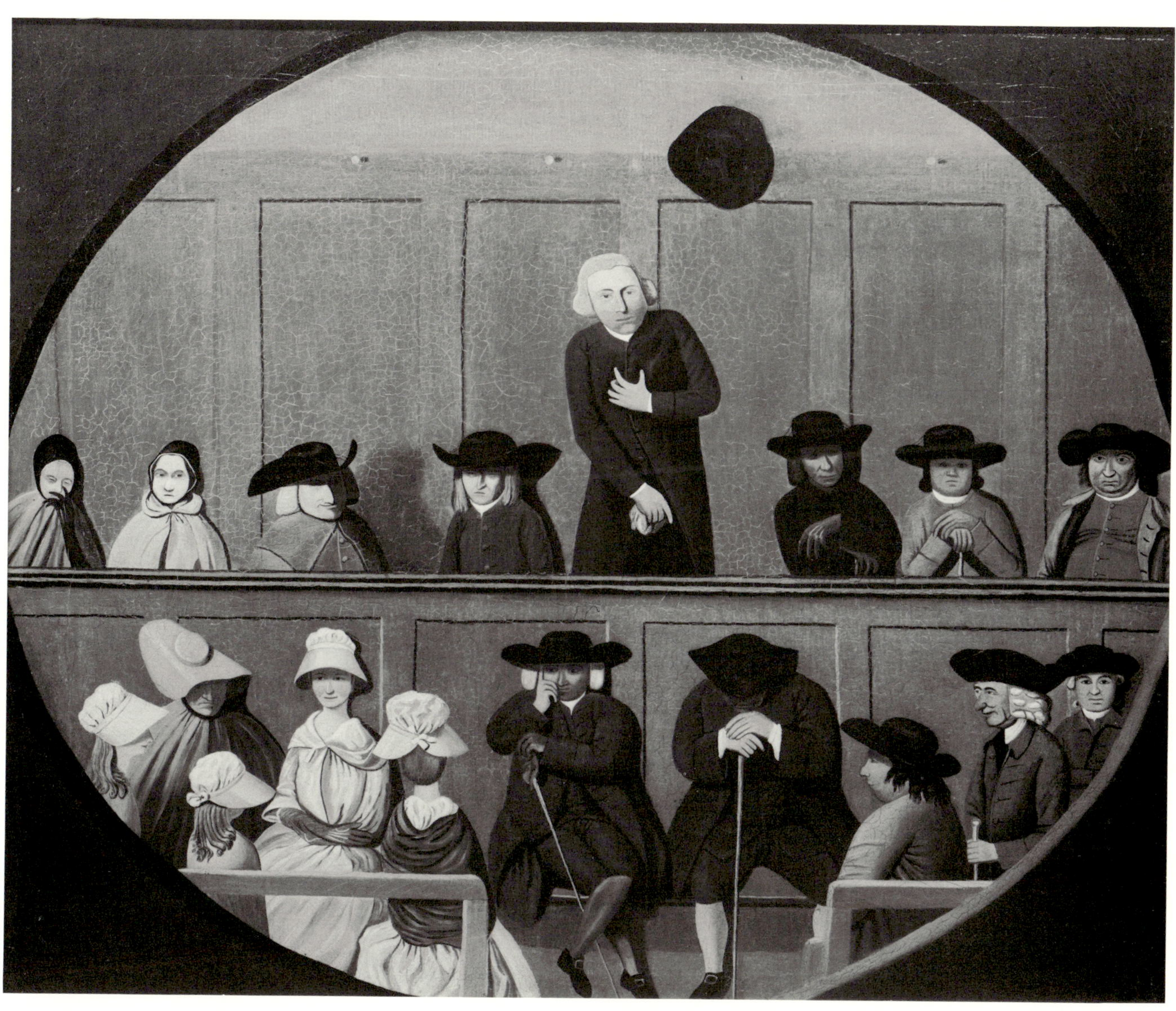

1. ANONYMOUS. *Quaker Meeting*, about 1790. 25 x 30 in. 64.456

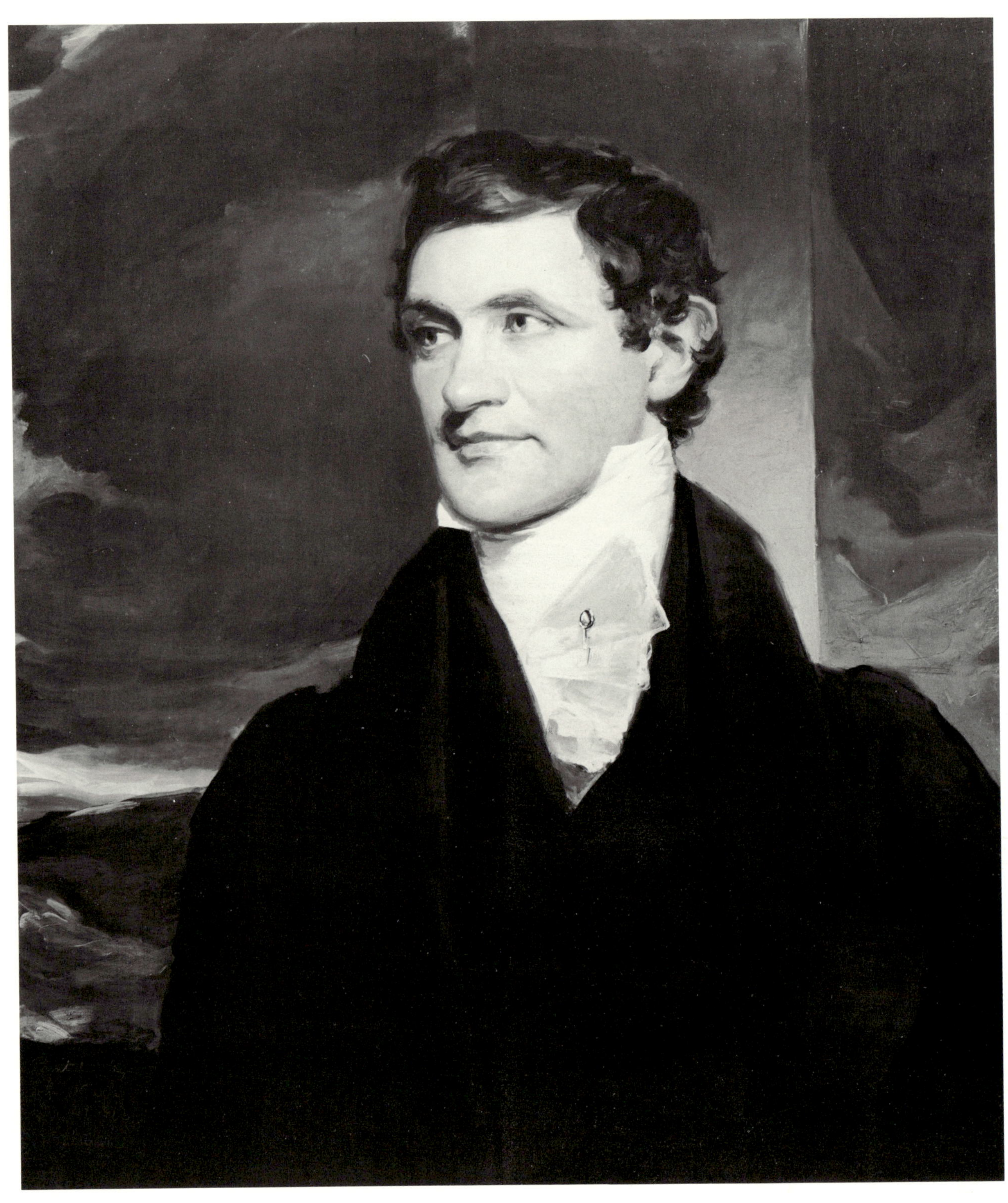

2. JOHN NEAGLE (1796–1860). *George Peabody*, 1822. 30 x 25 in. 48.462

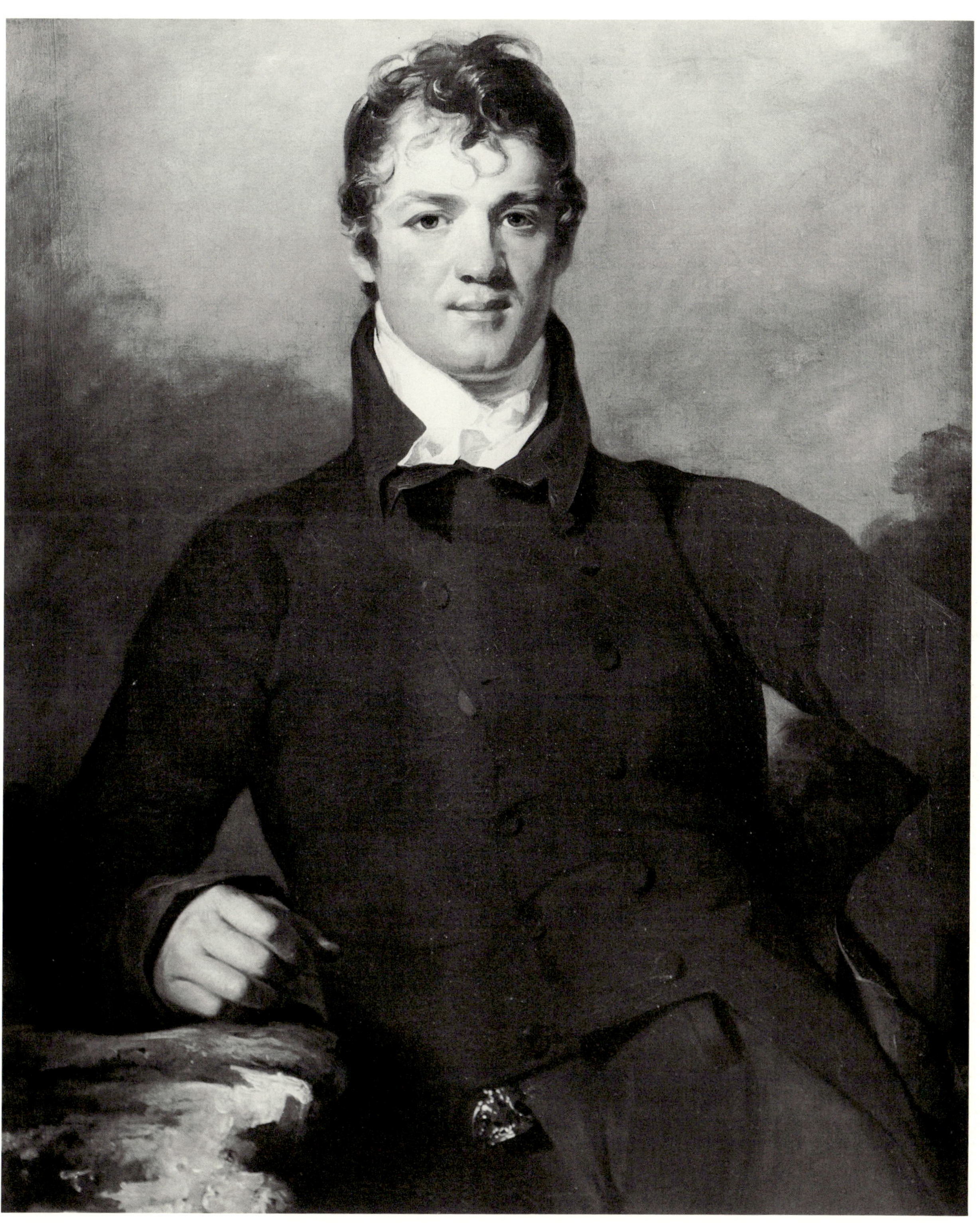

3. Thomas Sully (1783–1872). *John Myers*, 1814. 36 x 30 in. 45.894

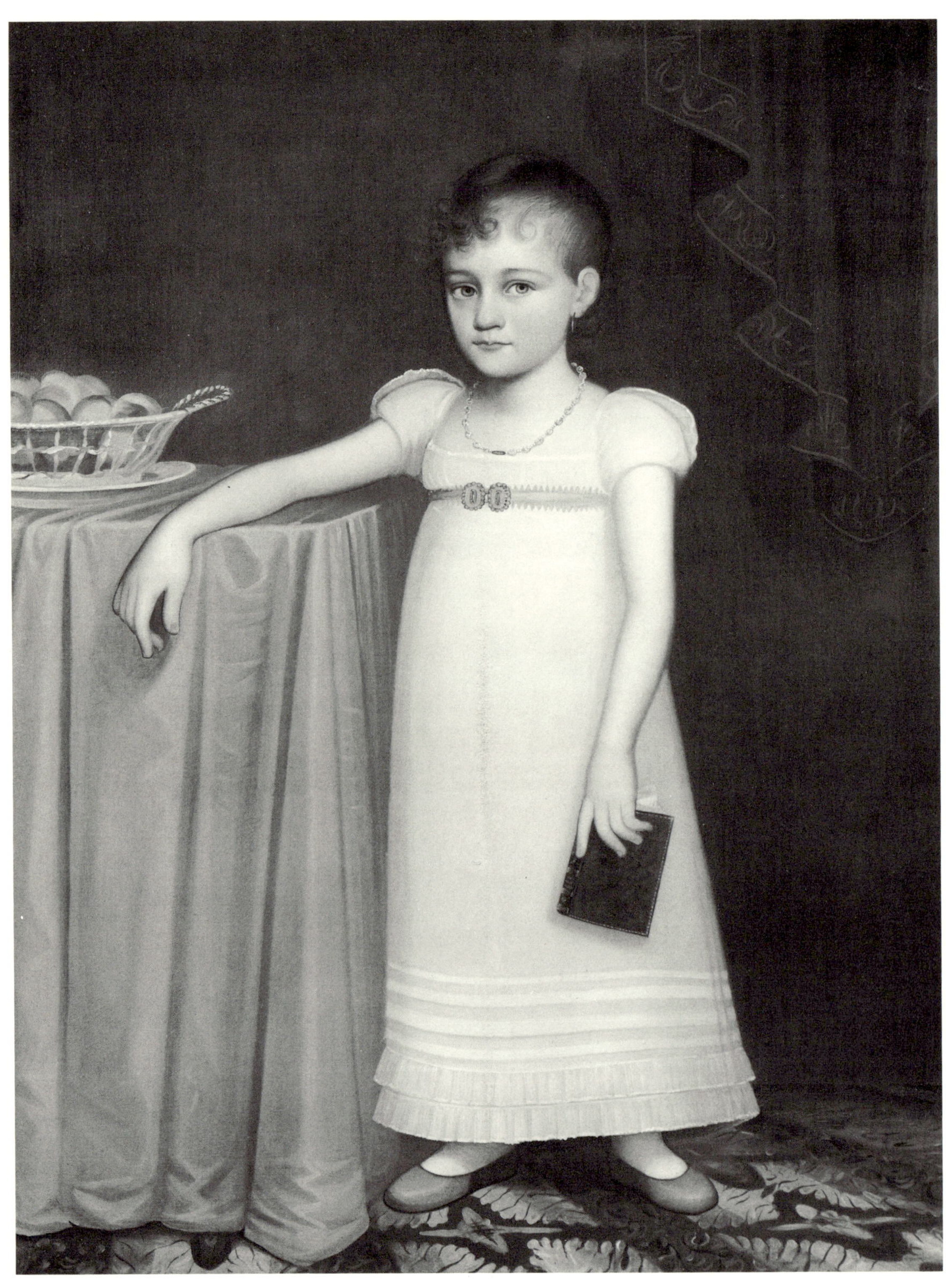

4. ANONYMOUS. *Phoebe Drake*, about 1815–1820. 48 x 36 in. 64.462

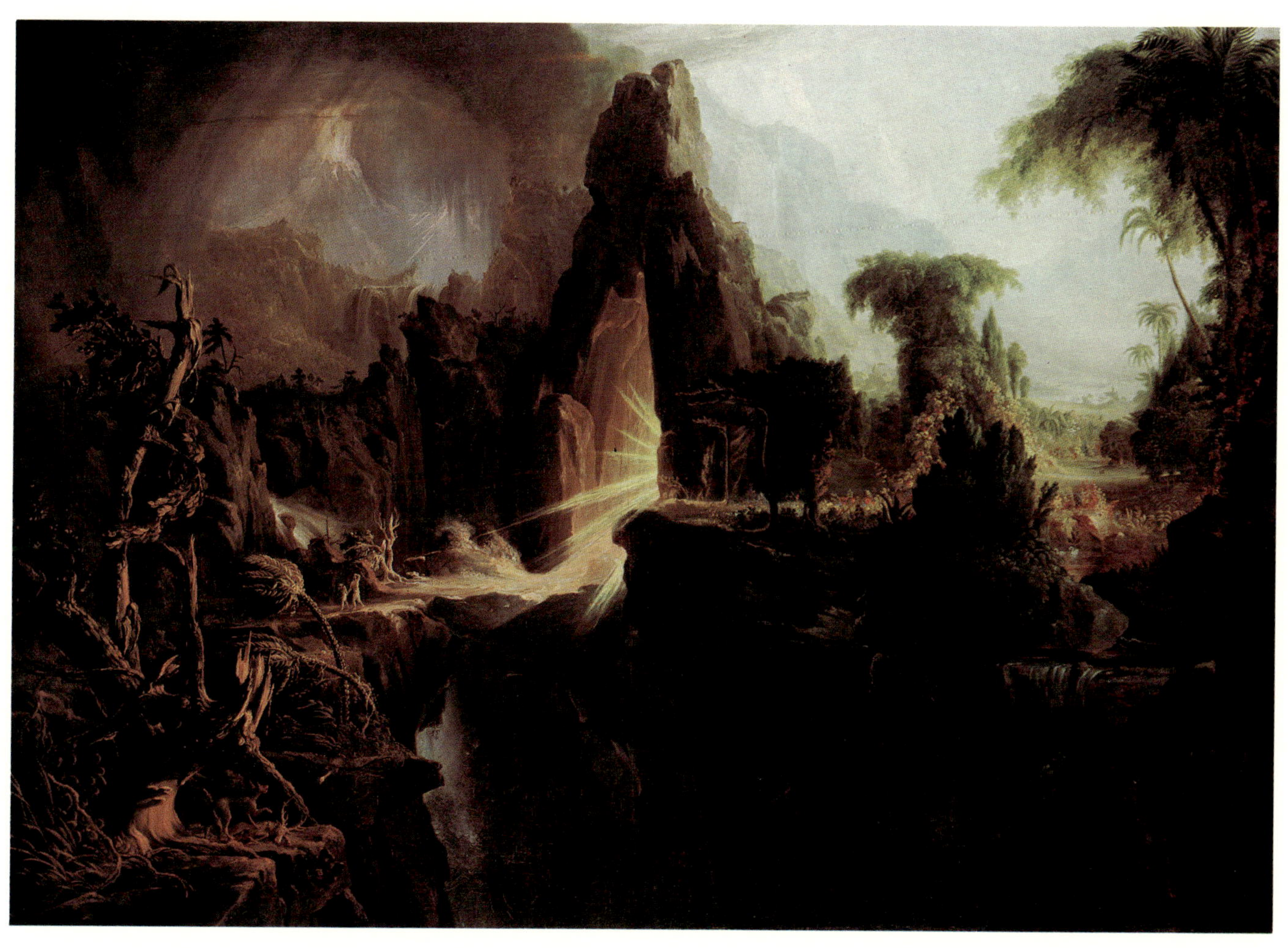

5. Thomas Cole (1801–1848). *Expulsion from the Garden of Eden*, about 1827–1828. 39 x 54 in. 47.1188

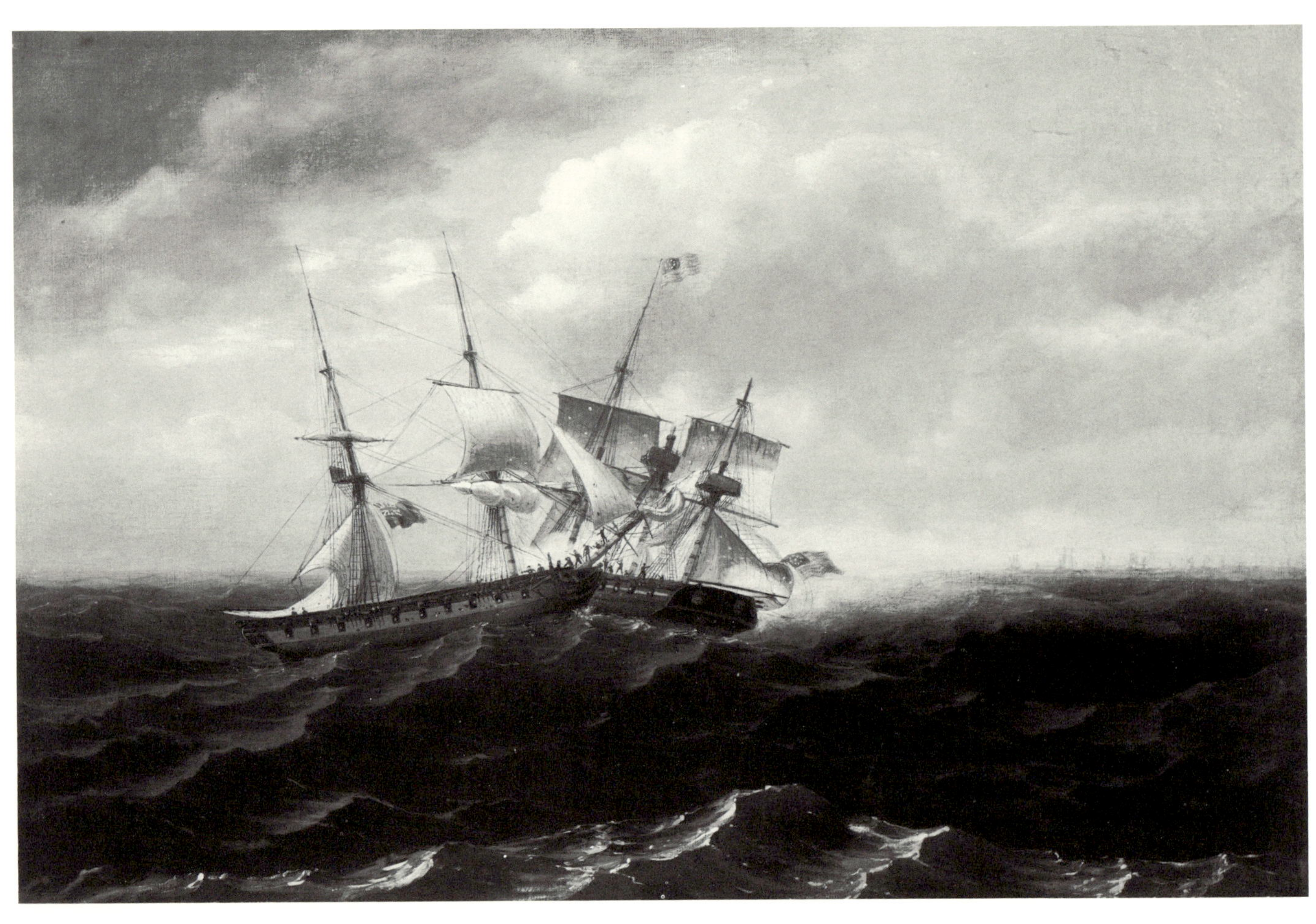

6. Thomas Birch (1779–1851). *The "Wasp" and the "Frolic"*, 1820. 20 x 30 in. 47.1186

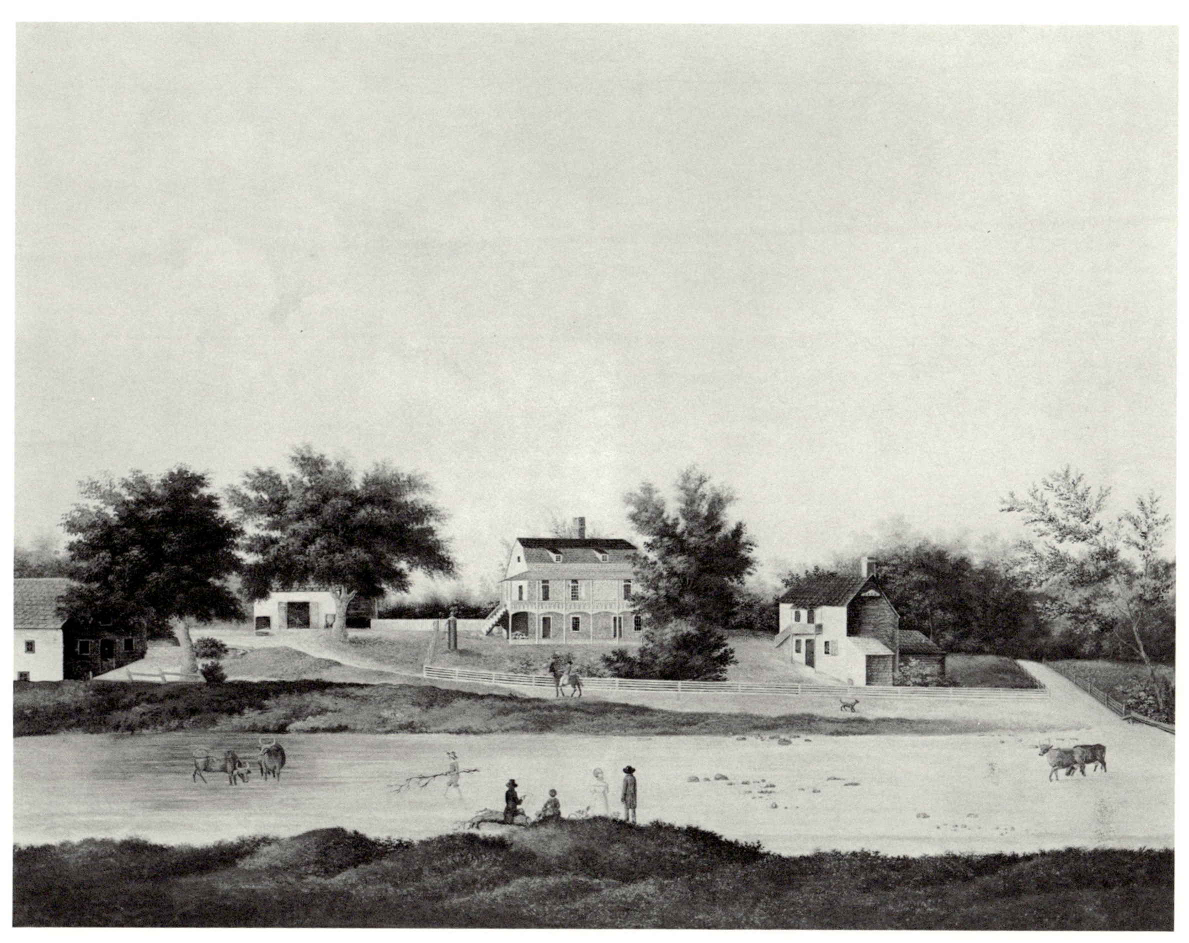

7. DIETZ. *Milford, North Wales, Pennsylvania*, about 1825–1833. 22 x 28½ in. 47.1209

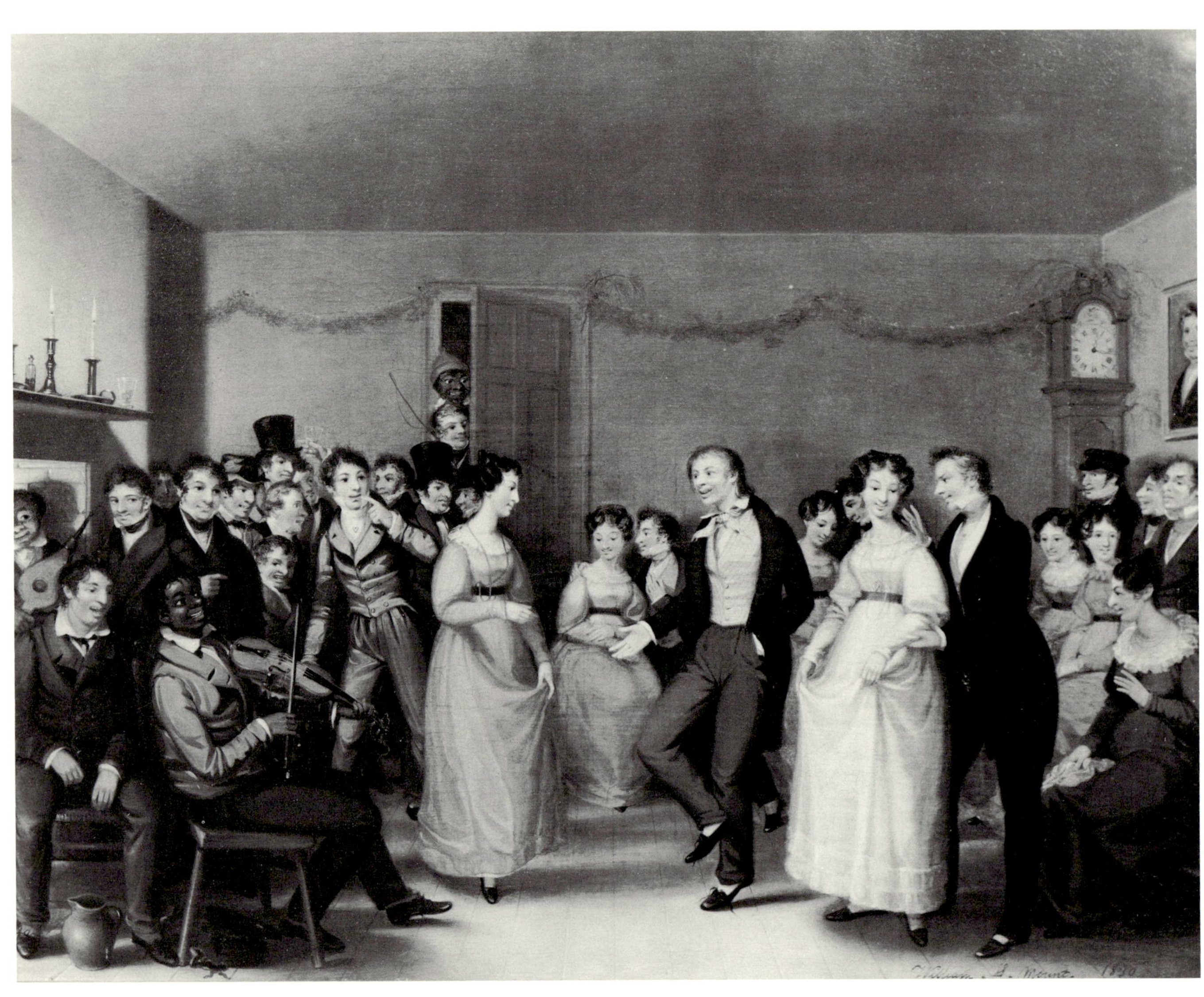

8. WILLIAM SIDNEY MOUNT (1807–1868). *Rustic Dance after a Sleigh Ride,* 1830. 22 x 27¼ in. 48.458

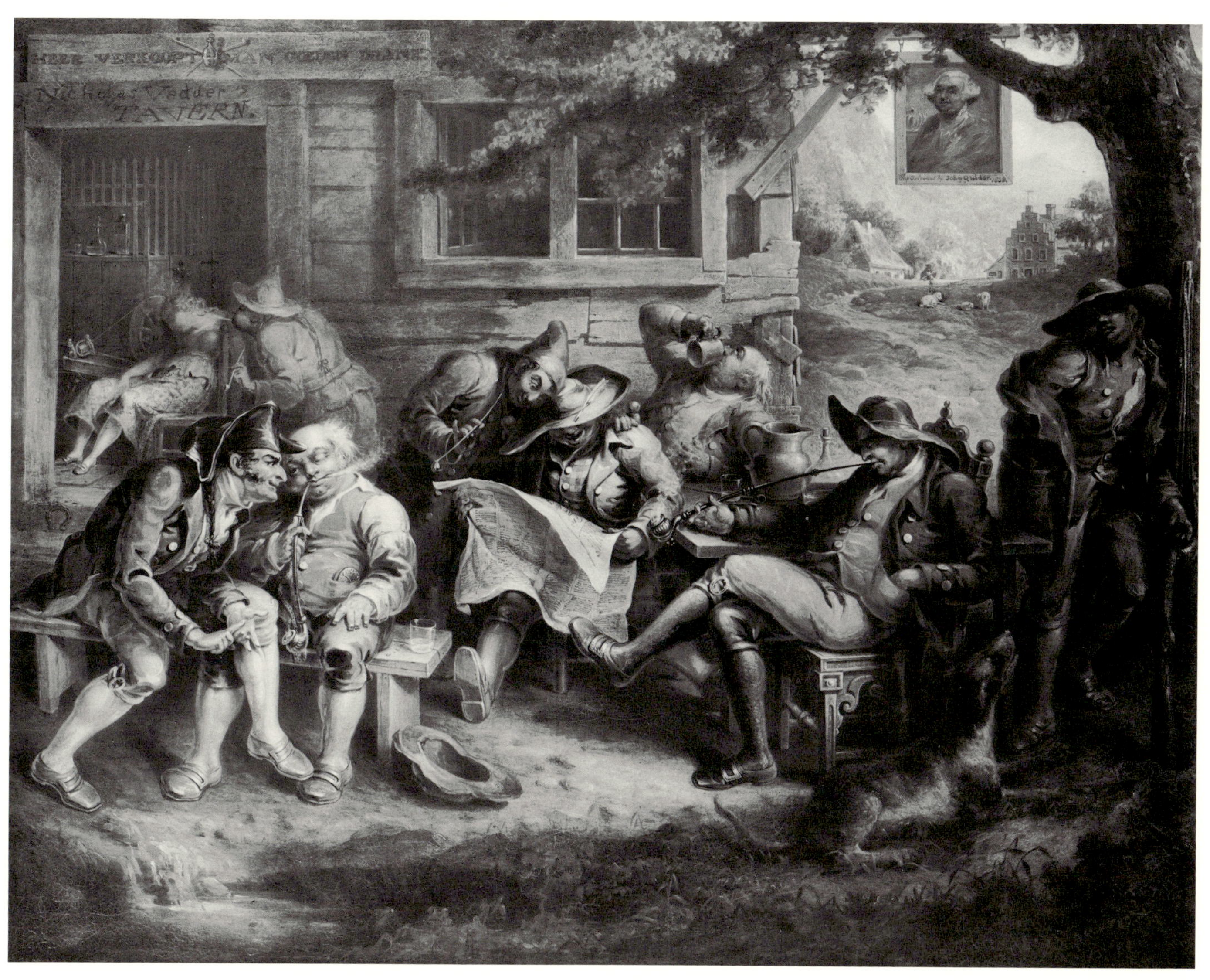

9. JOHN QUIDOR (1801–1881). *Rip Van Winkle at Nicholas Vedder's Tavern*, 1839. 27 x 34 in. 48.469

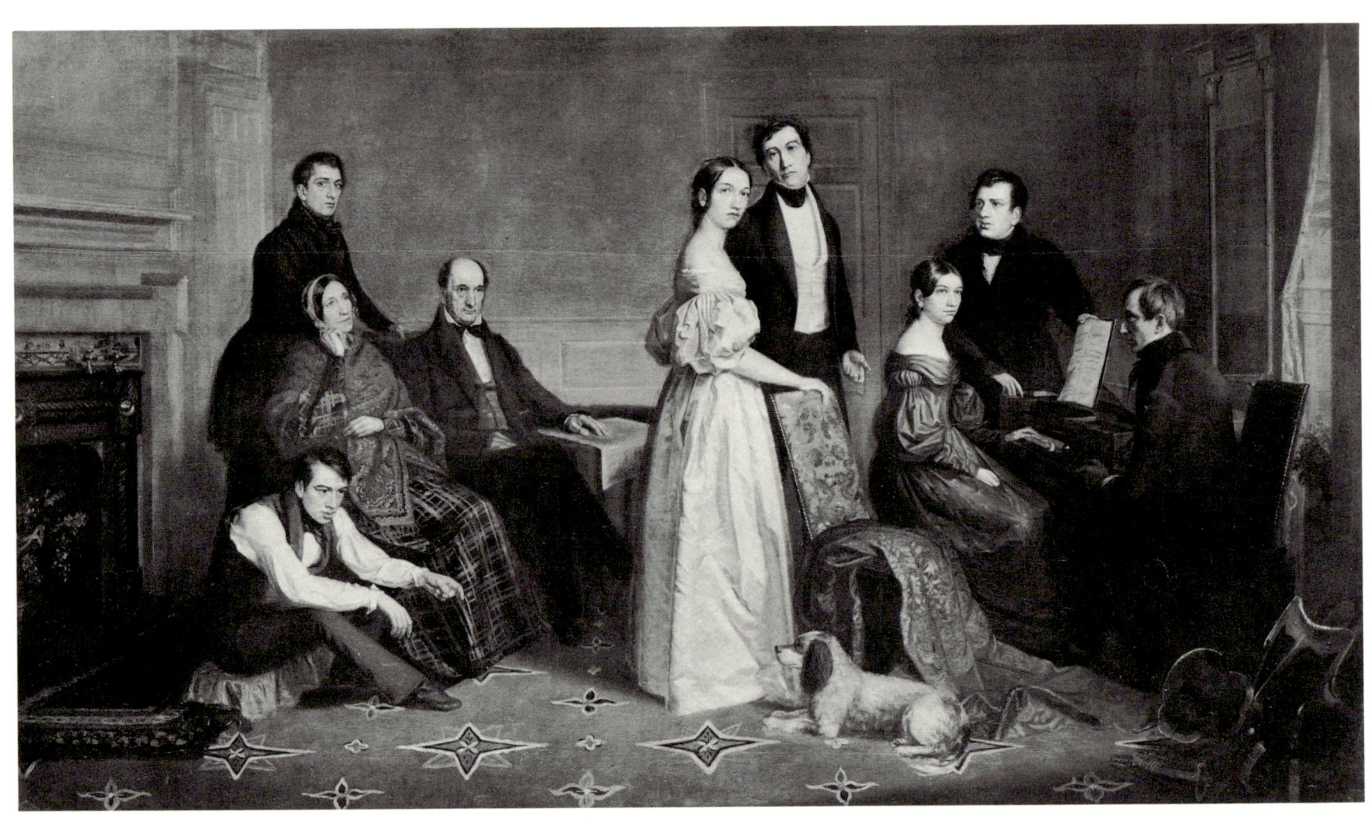

10. George Hollingsworth (1813–1882).
The Hollingsworth Family, about 1840. 42 x 72 in. 47.1227

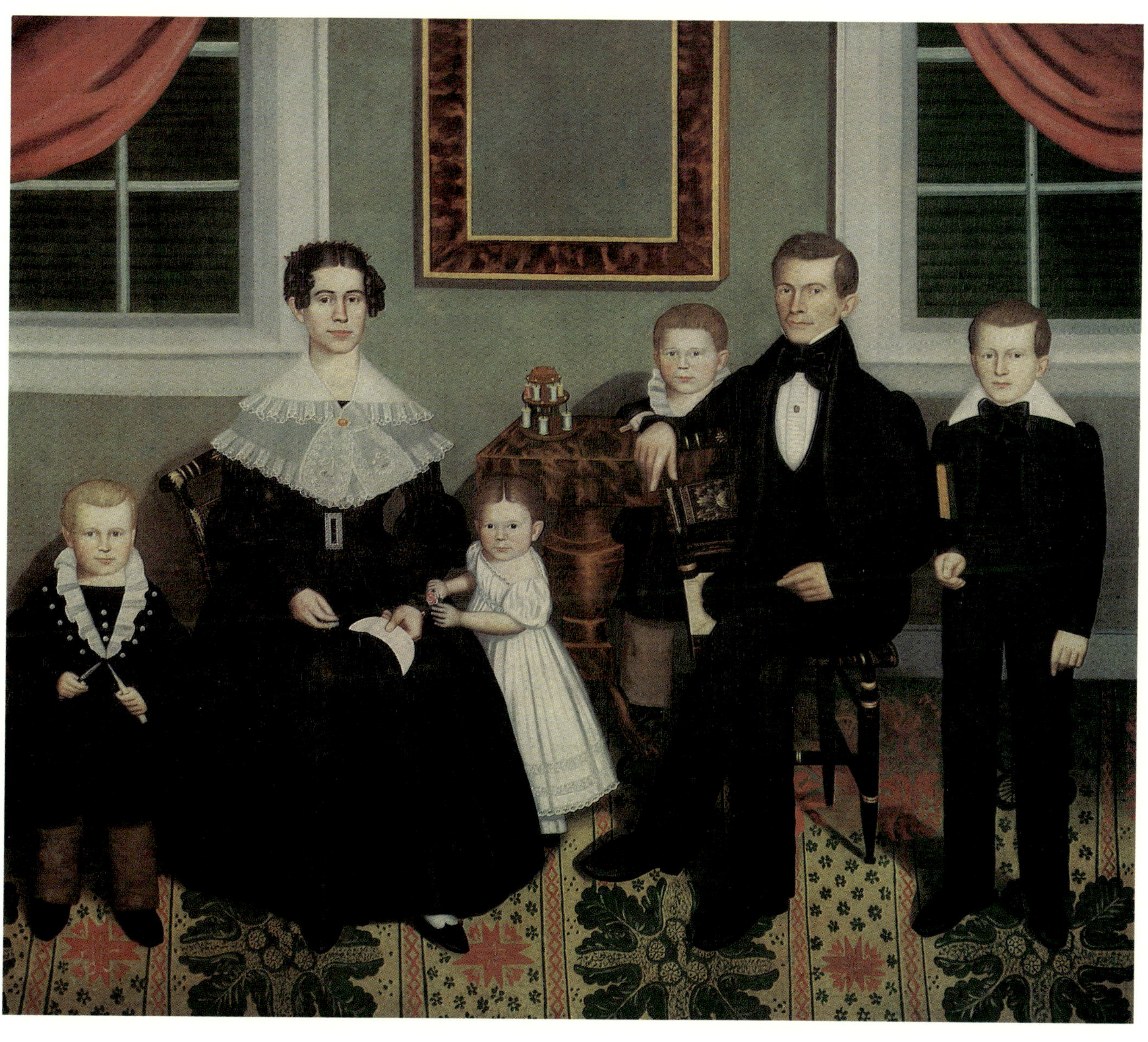

11. ERASTUS SALISBURY FIELD (1805–1900).
Joseph Moore and His Family, 1839, 82¾ x 93¼ in. 58.25

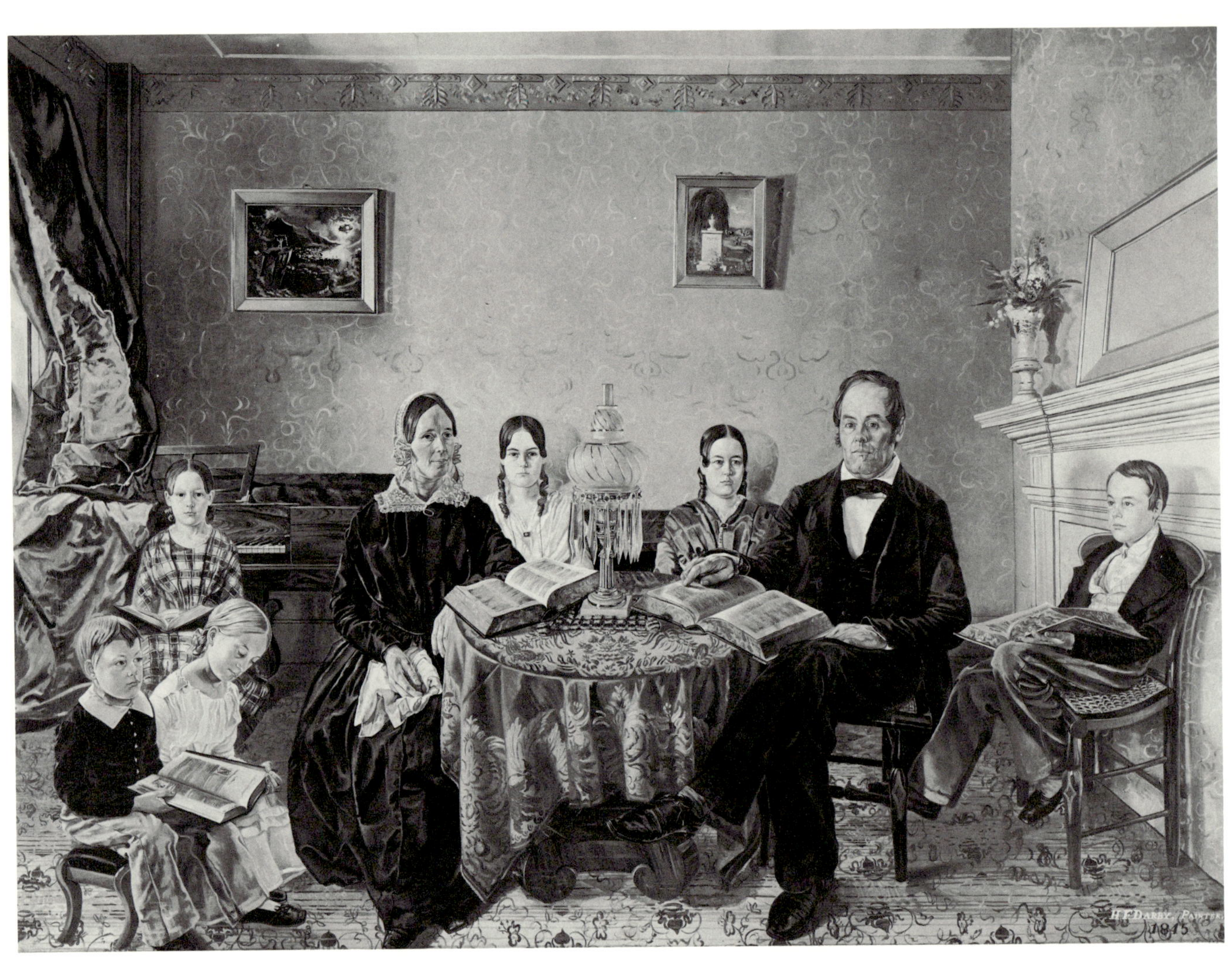

12. Henry F. Darby (1829–1897).
The Reverend John Atwood and His Family, 1845. 72 x 96¼ in. 62.269

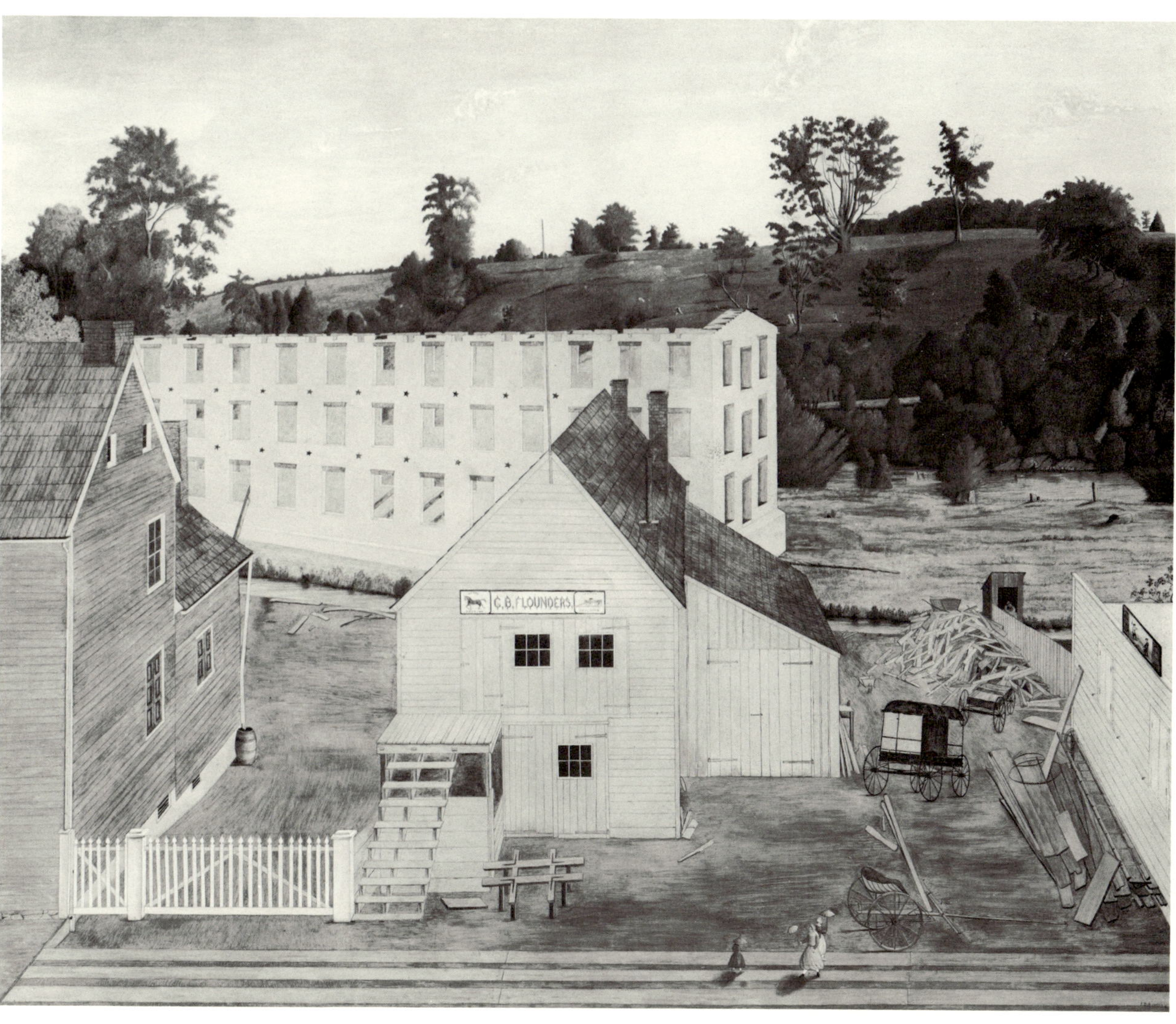

13. J. D. Bunting. *View of Darby, Pennsylvania, after the Burning of Lord's Mill*, about 1840–1850.
42 x 51¼ in. 62.264

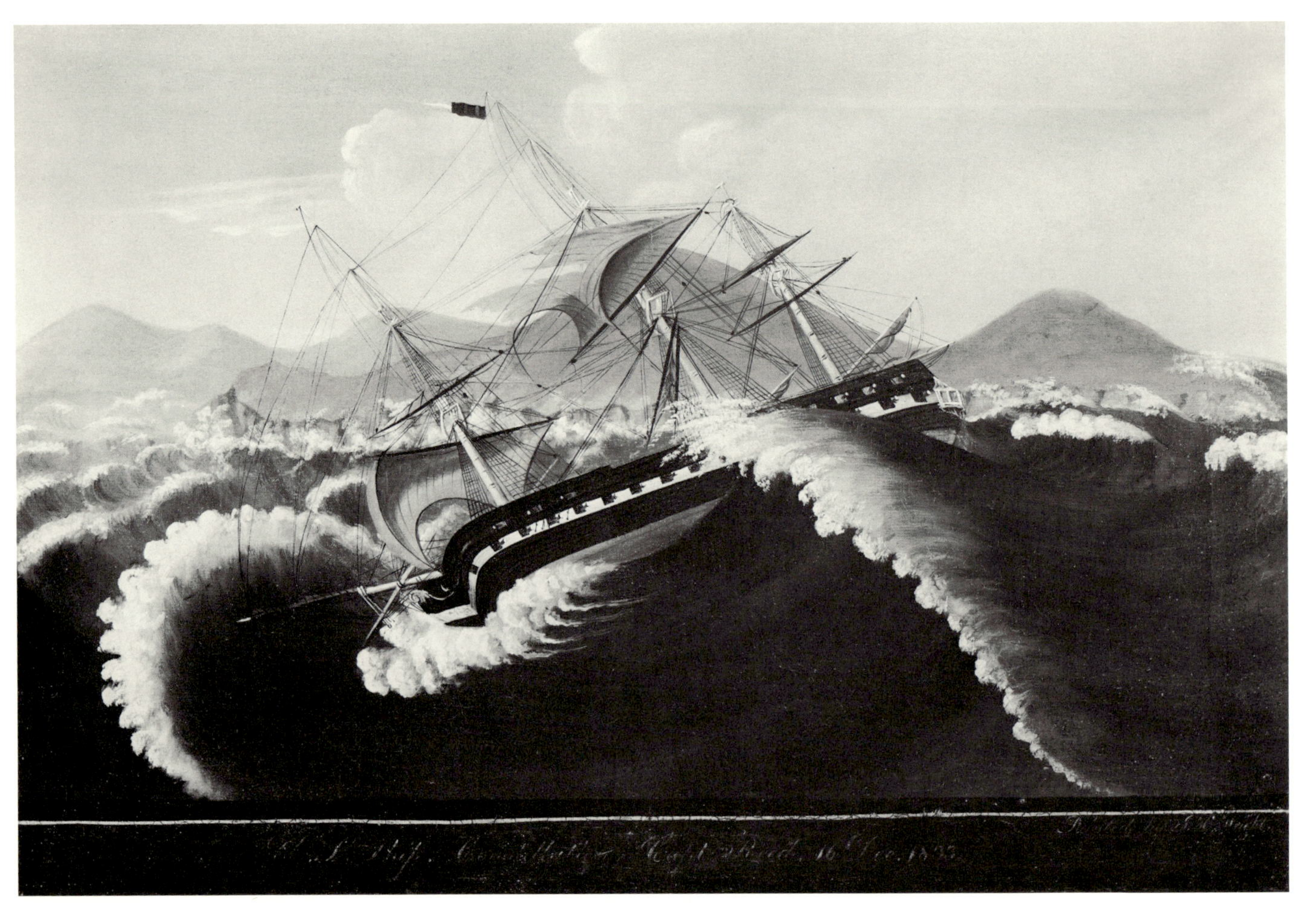

14. JAMES HENRY WRIGHT (1813–1883). *U.S. Ship "Constellation"*, 1833. 20 x 30 in. 48.495

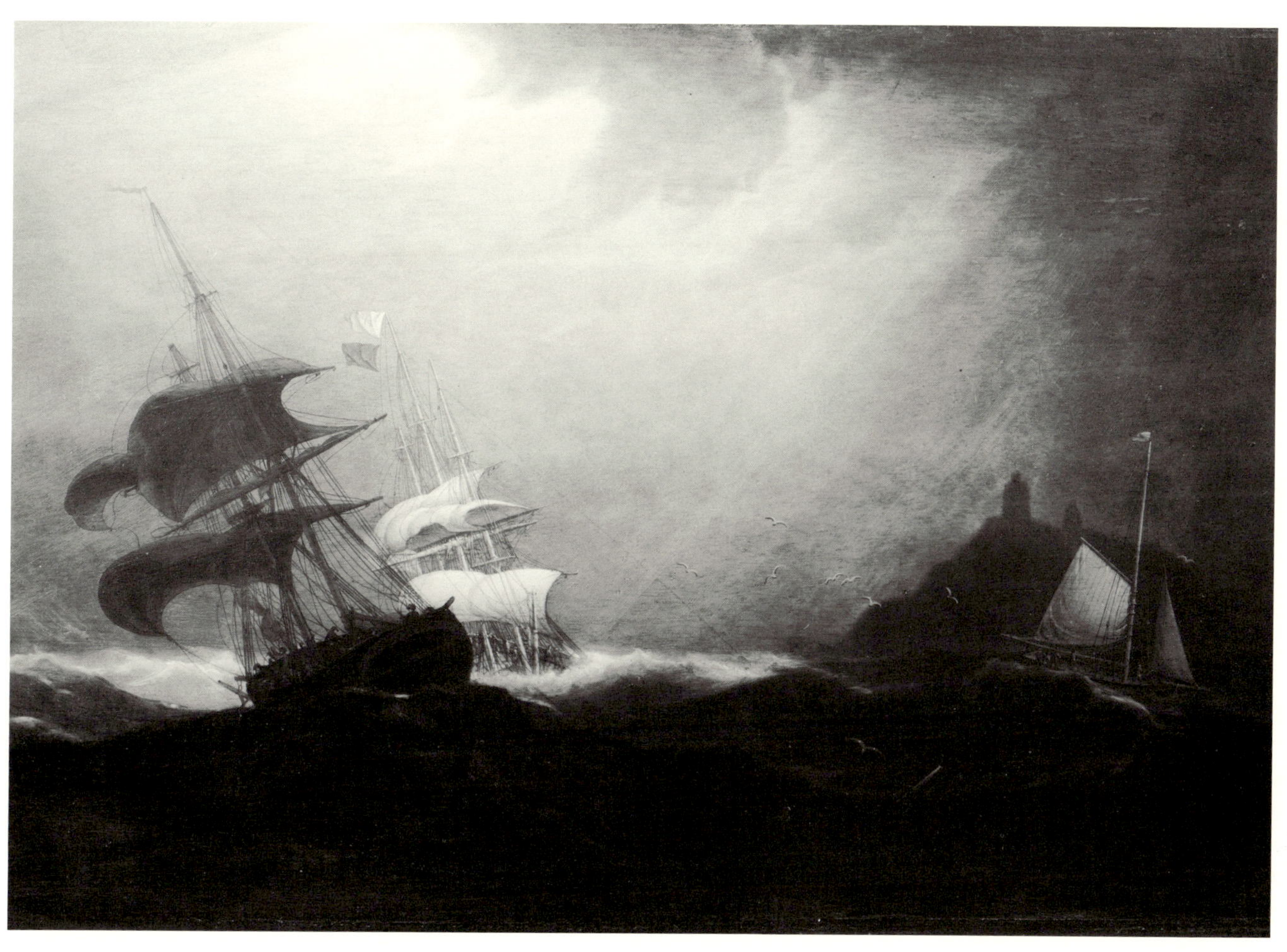

15. Robert Salmon (1775 – about 1845). *Storm at Sea*, 1840. 16½ x 24¼ in. 48.473

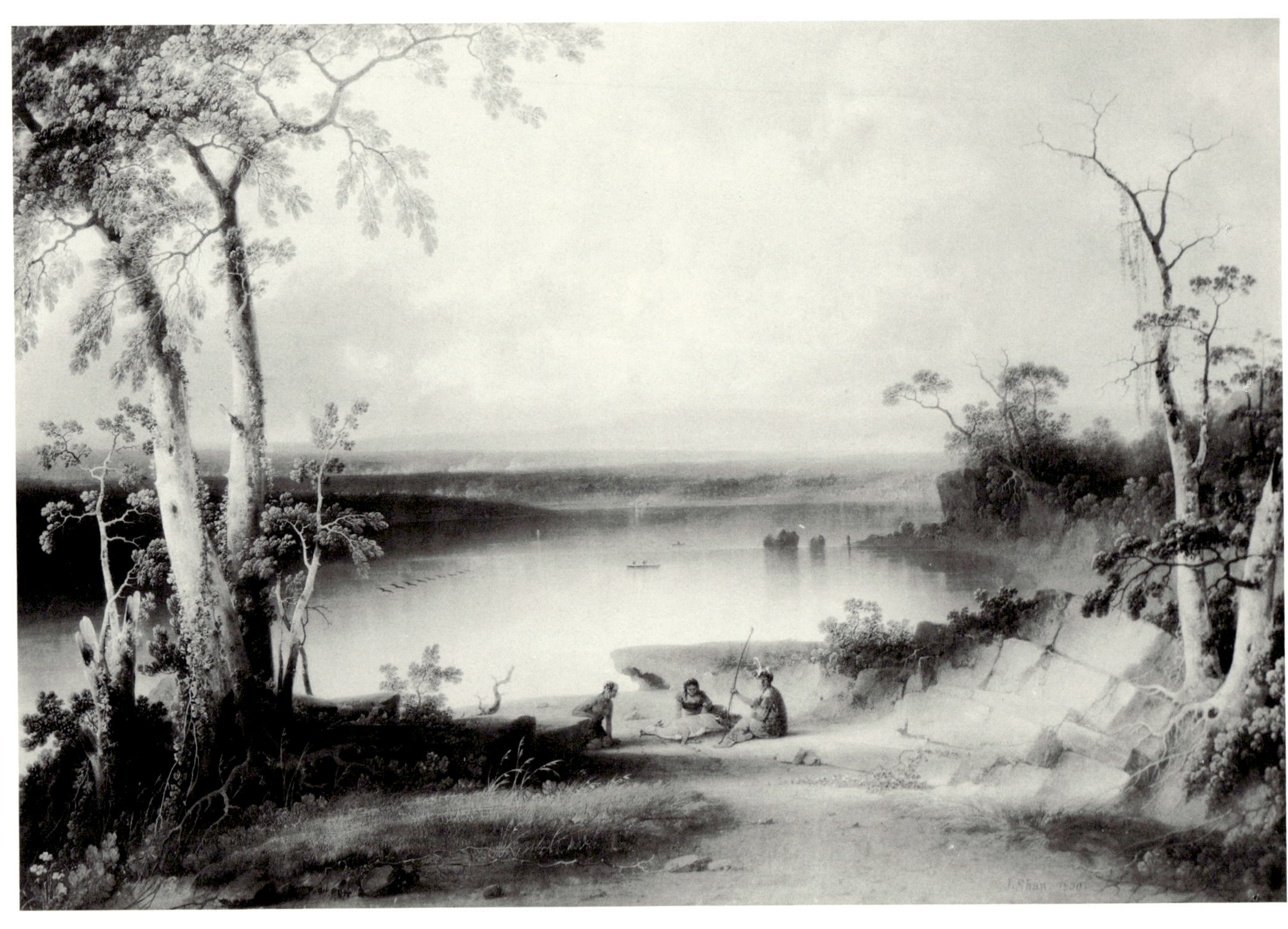

16. Joshua Shaw (1776–1860). *On the Susquehanna*, 1839. 39 x 55½ in. 48.476

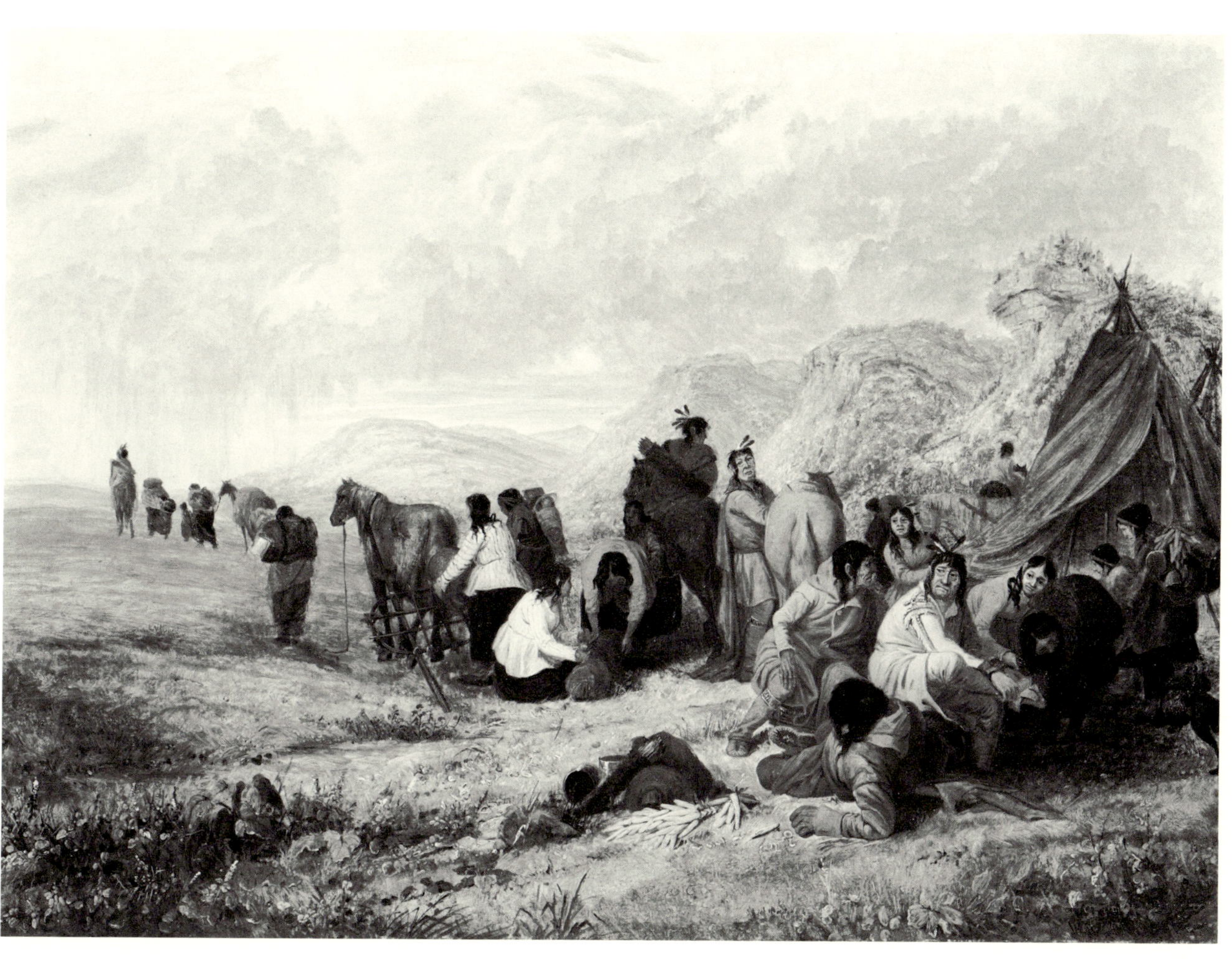

17. Seth Eastman (1808–1875). *Sioux Indians Breaking up Camp*, before 1848. 25½ x 35 in. 46.850

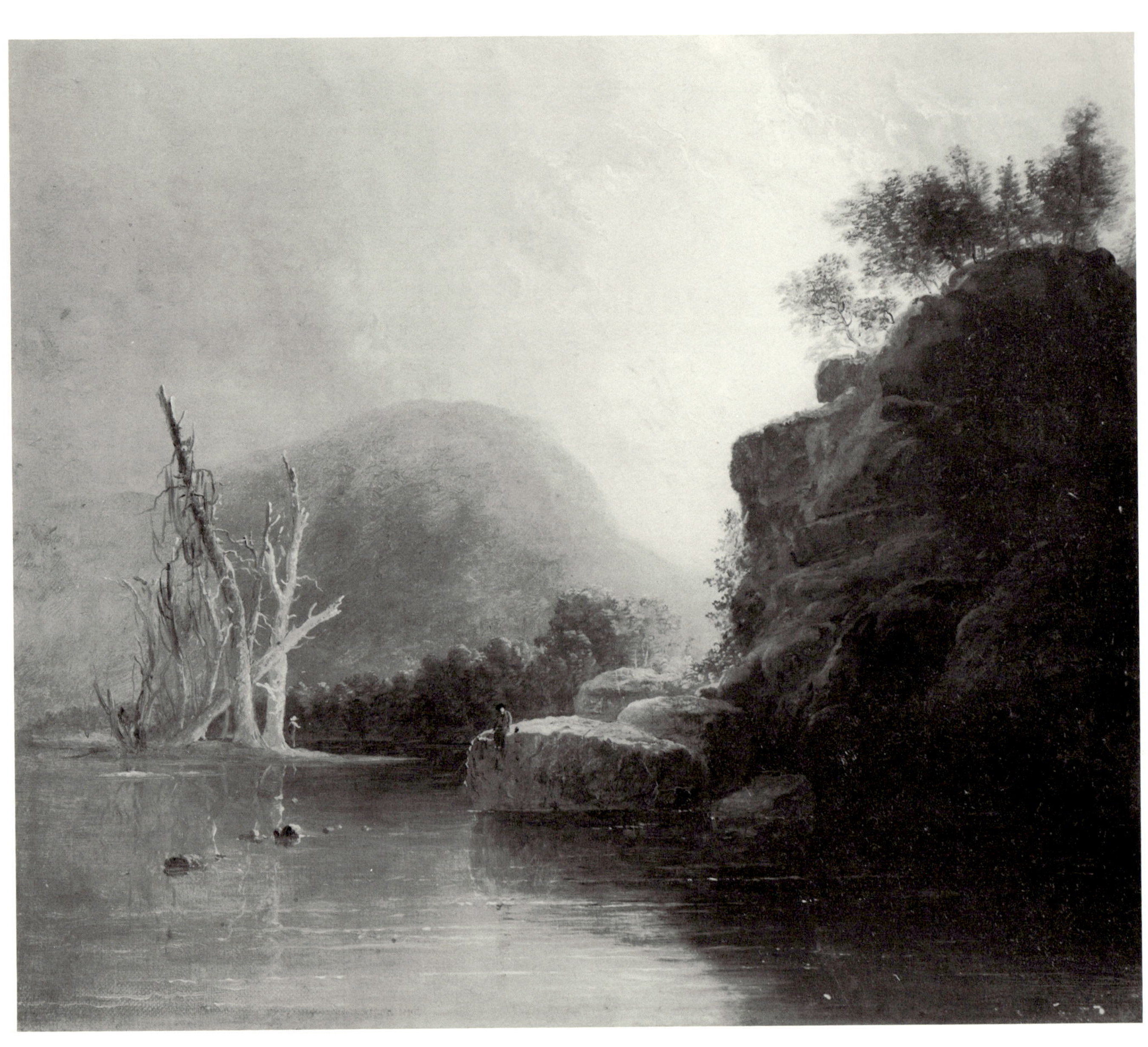

18. Thomas Doughty (1793–1856). *Two Men Fishing in a Mountain Lake*, 1837. 14 x 16 in. 64.596

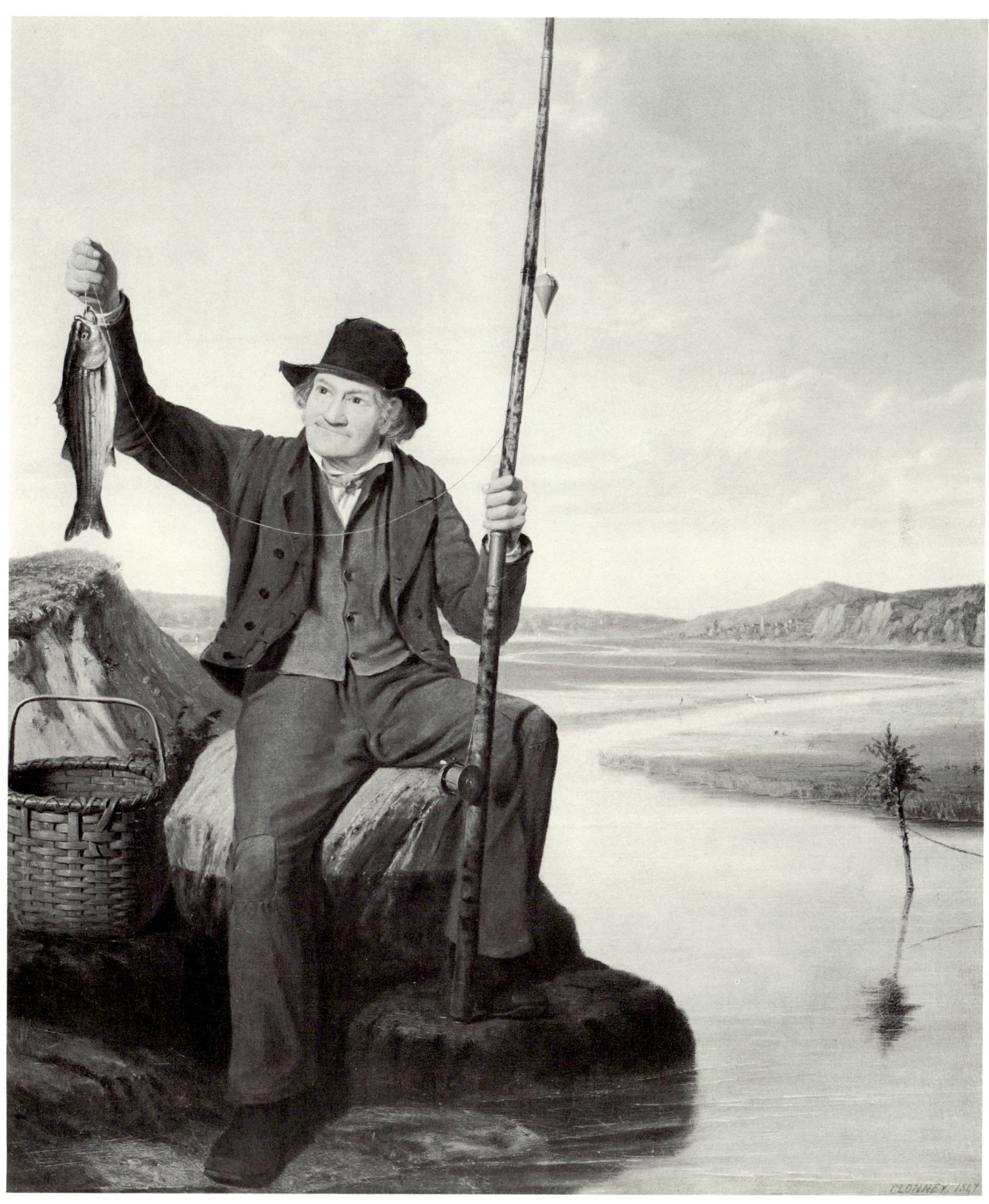

19. James Goodwyn Clonney (1812–1867). *The Happy Moment*, 1847. 27 x 22 in. 47.1222

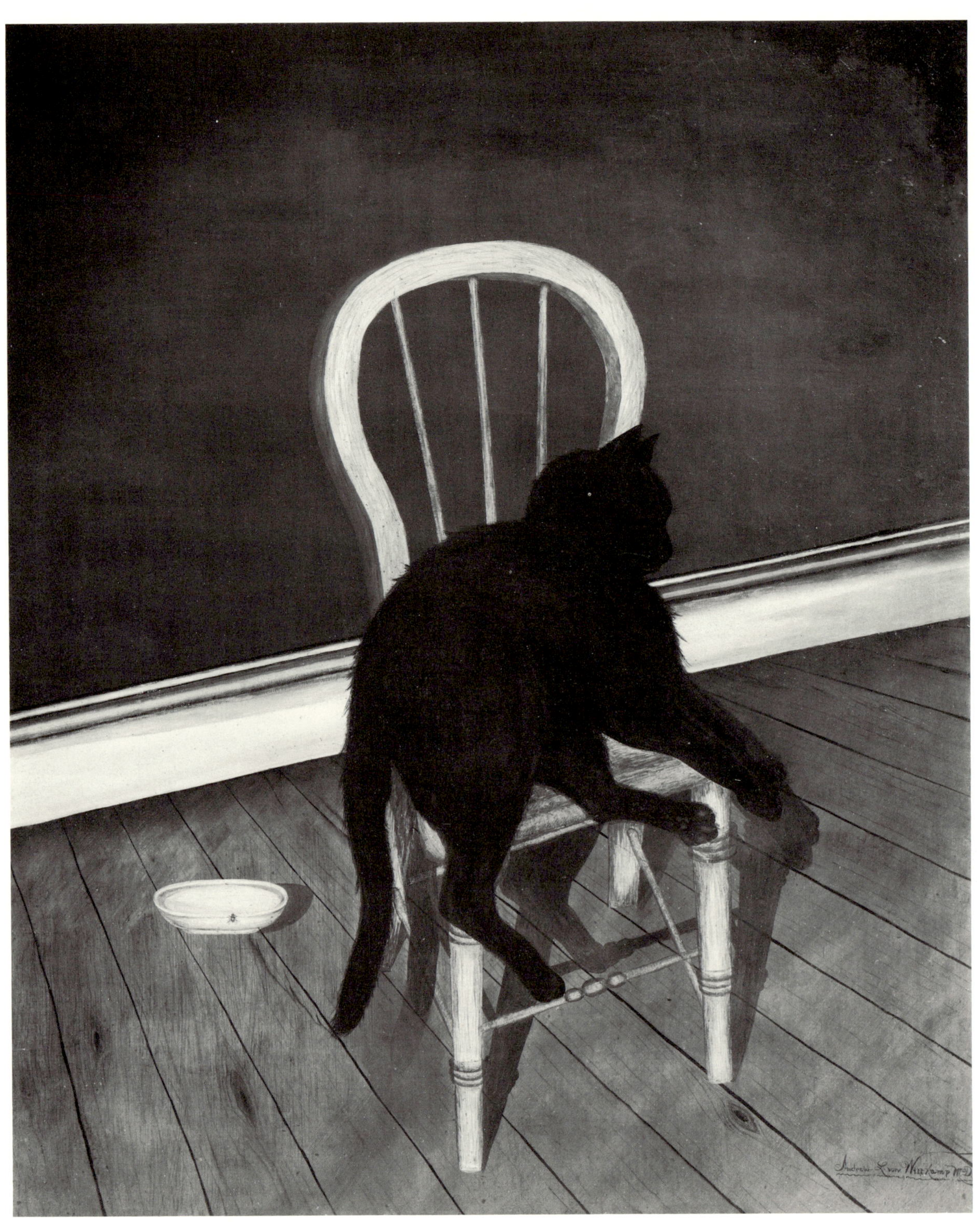

20. ANDREW L. VON WITTKAMP. *Black Cat on a Chair.* 36 x 29¼ in. 48.494

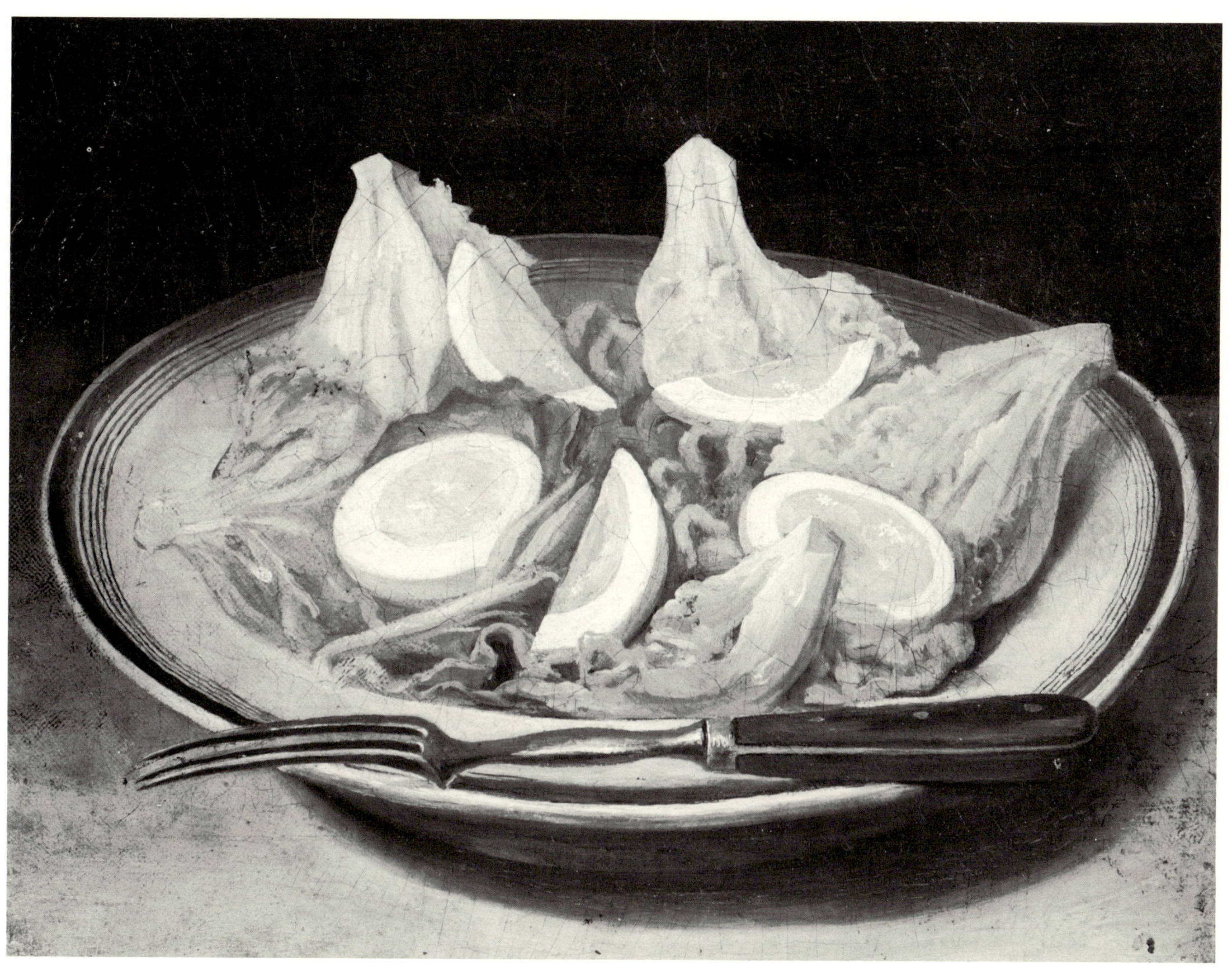

21. ANONYMOUS. *Egg Salad*, about 1840. 8½ x 11 in. 47.1220

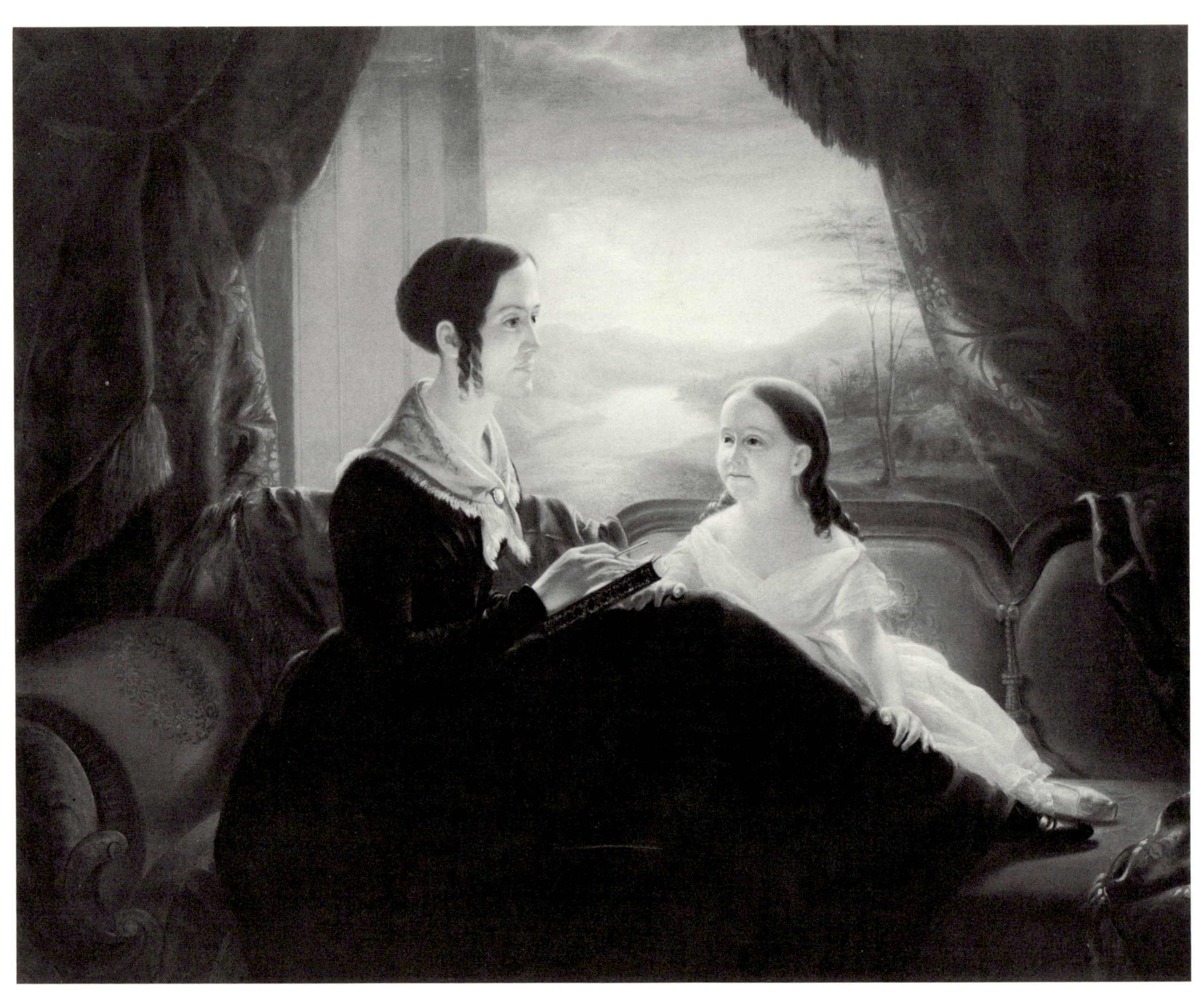

22. Jeremiah Pearson Hardy (1800–1887).
Catharine Wheeler Hardy and Her Daughter, about 1842. 29¼ x 36 in. 47.1146

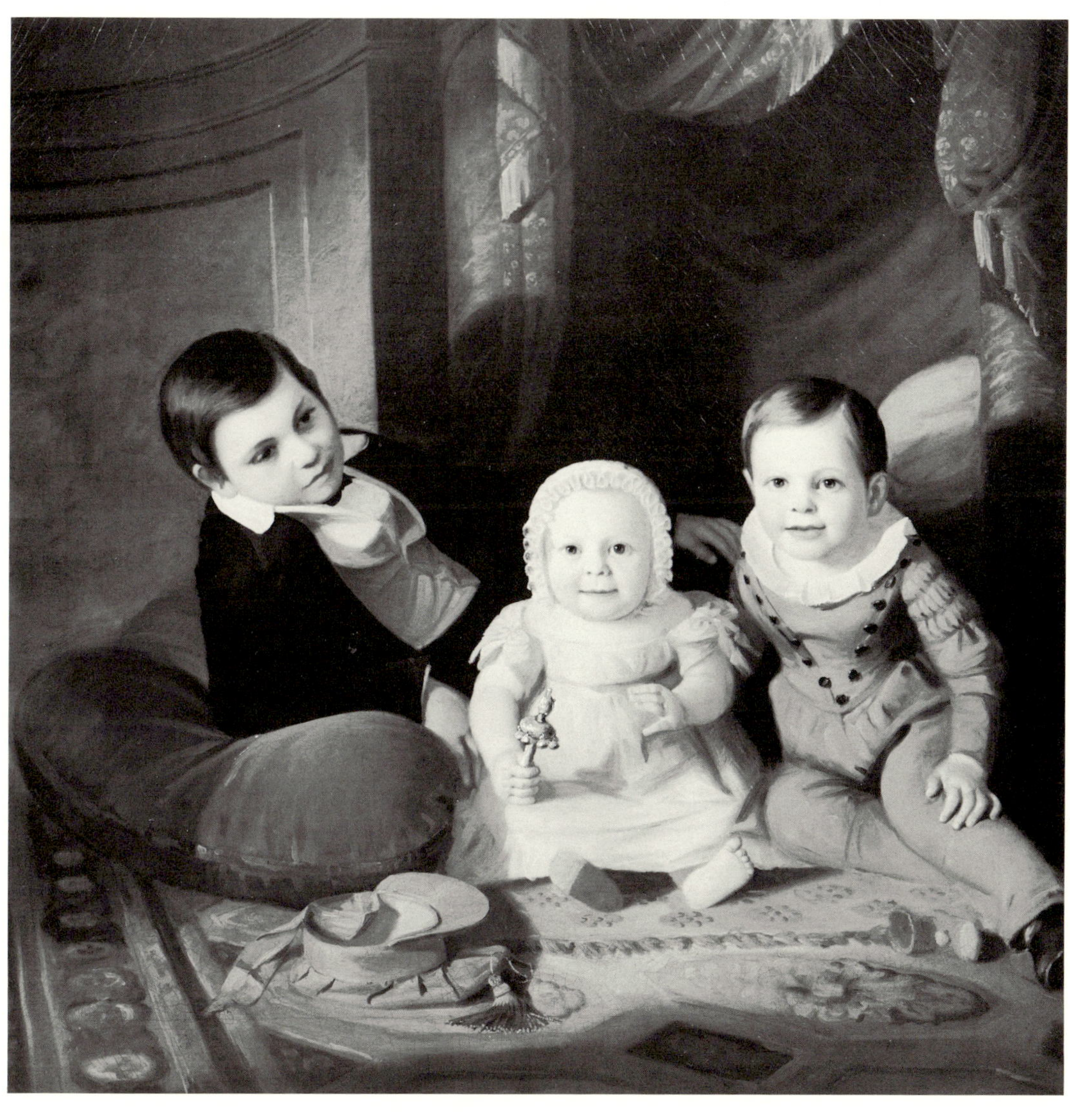

23. JOHN F. FRANCIS (about 1810–1885). *Three Children*, 1840. 42 x 42 in. 47.1142

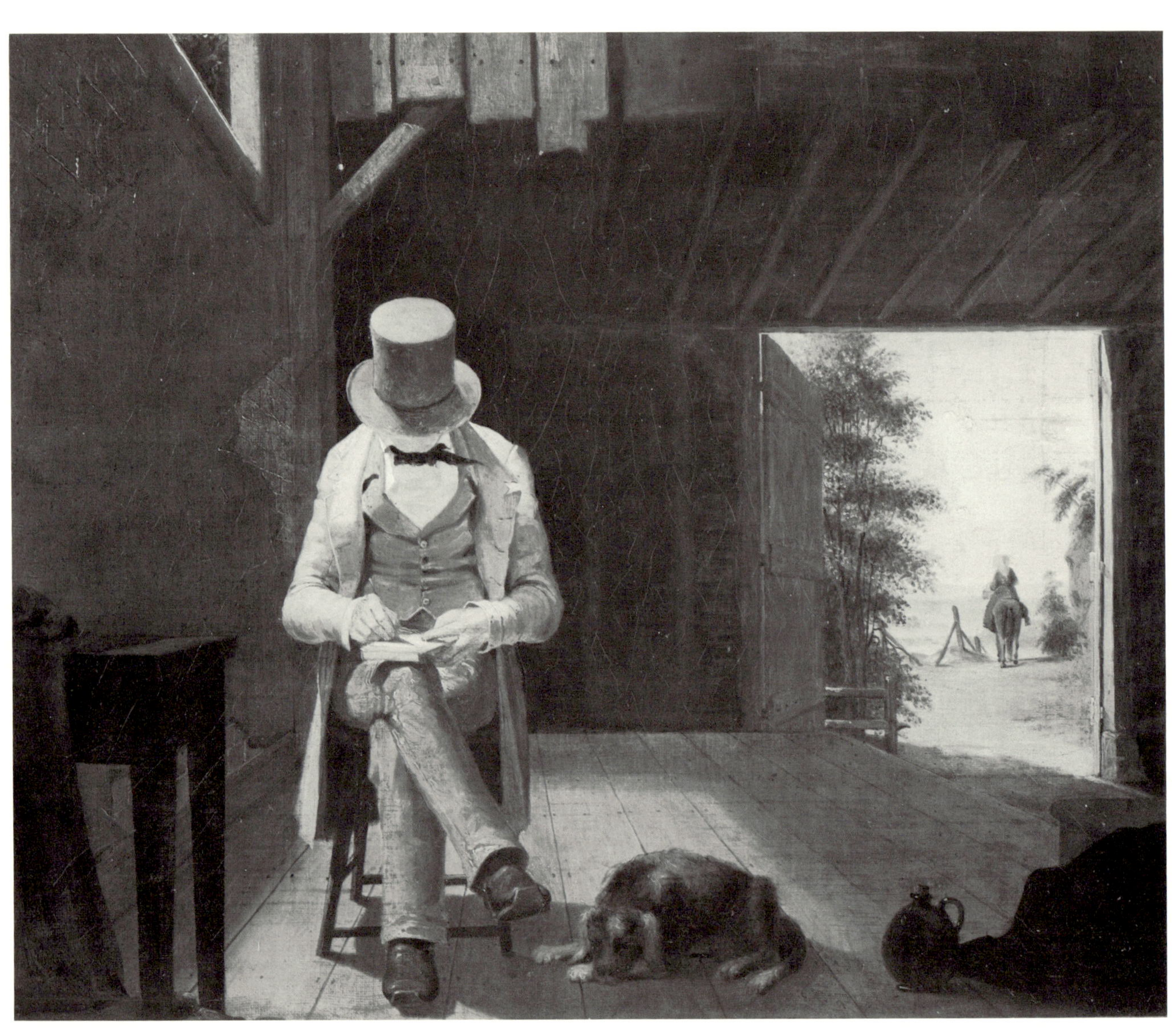

24. THOMAS HICKS (1823–1890). *Calculating,* 1844. 14 x 16¾ in. 62.273

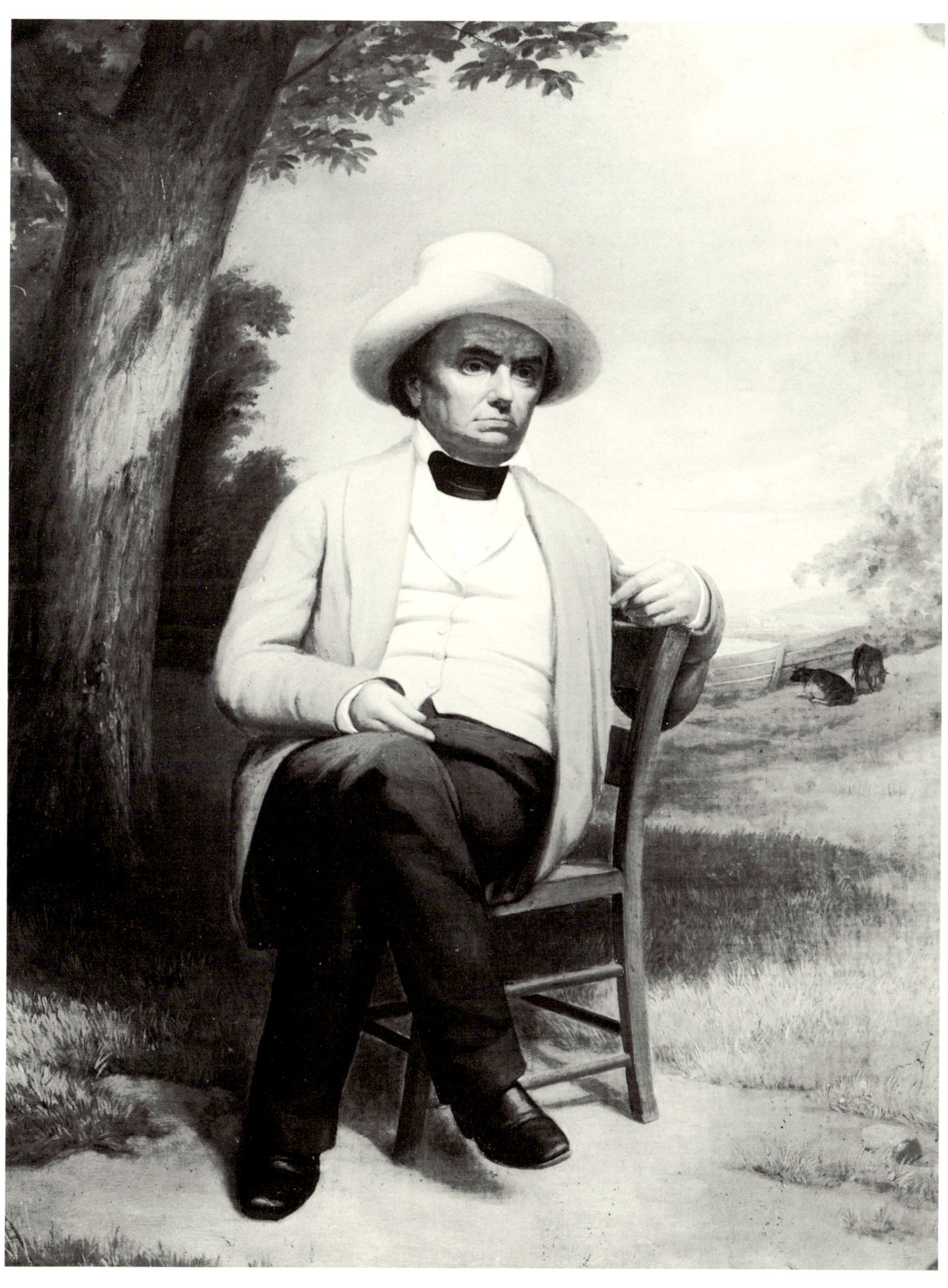

25. **Anonymous**. *Daniel Webster at His Farm*, about 1840–1845. 26 x 20 in. 47.1211

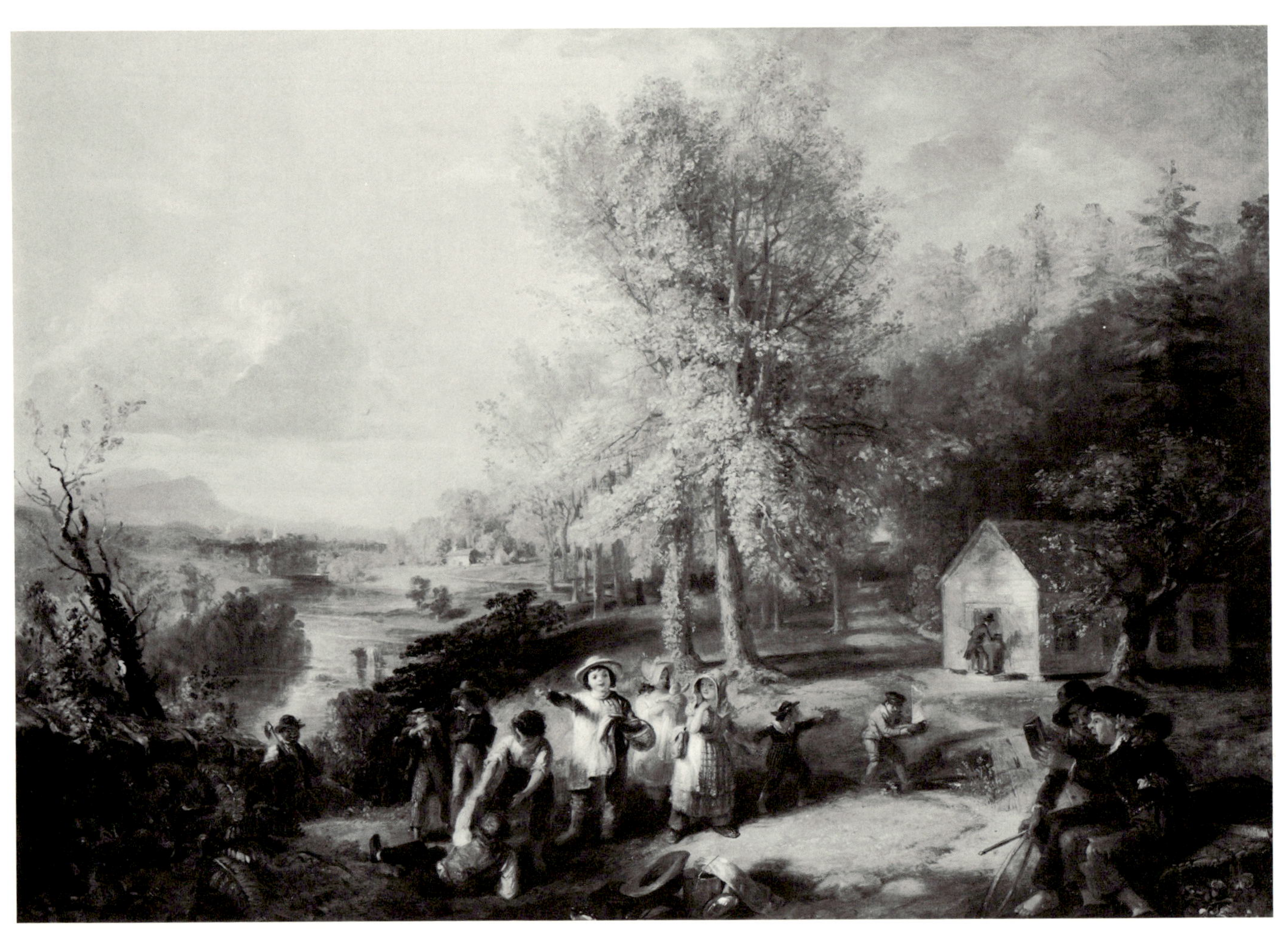

26. Henry Inman (1801–1846).
Dismissal of School on an October Afternoon, 1845. 26 x 36 in. 48.432

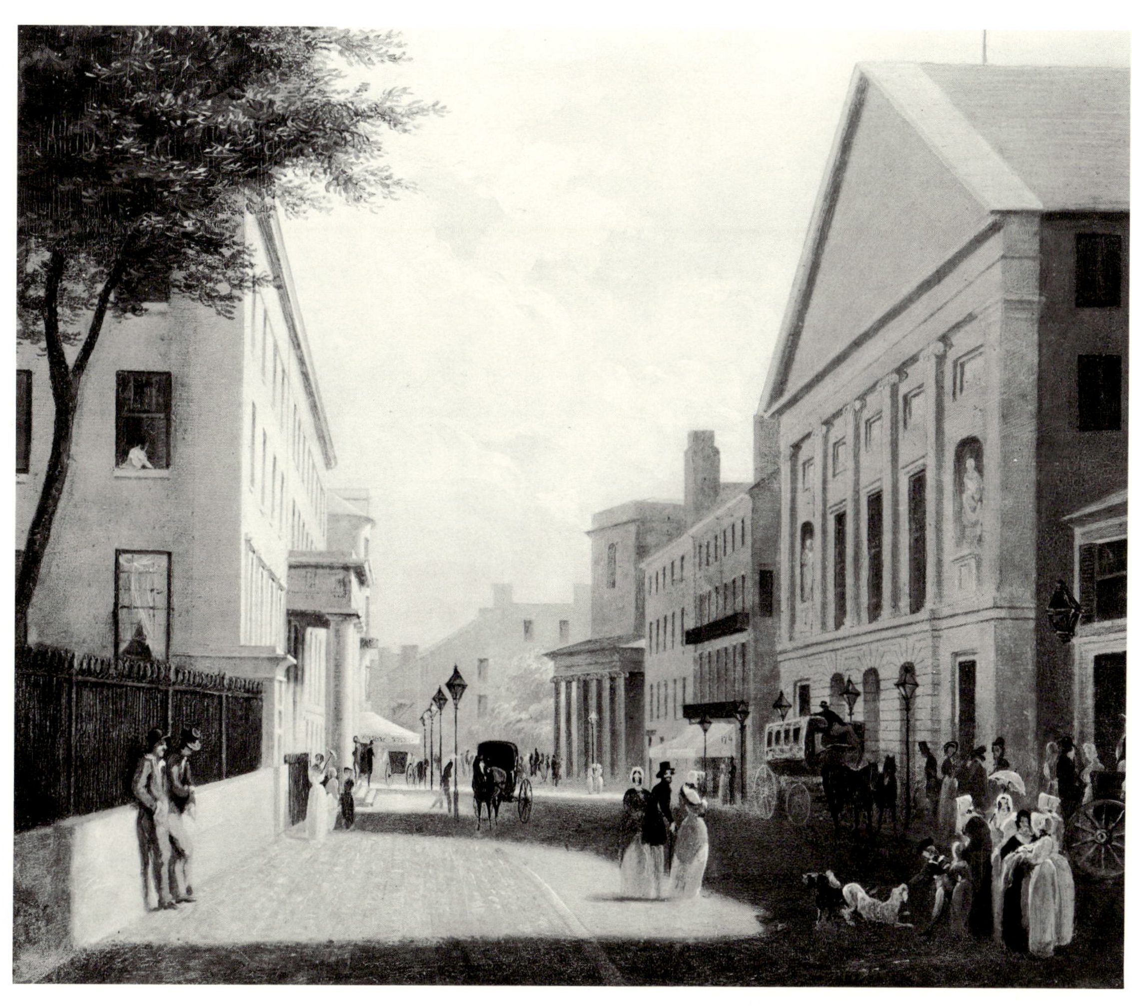

27. PHILIP HARRY (active 1843–1847). *Tremont Street, Boston*, before 1843. 13¾ x 16 in. 47.1150

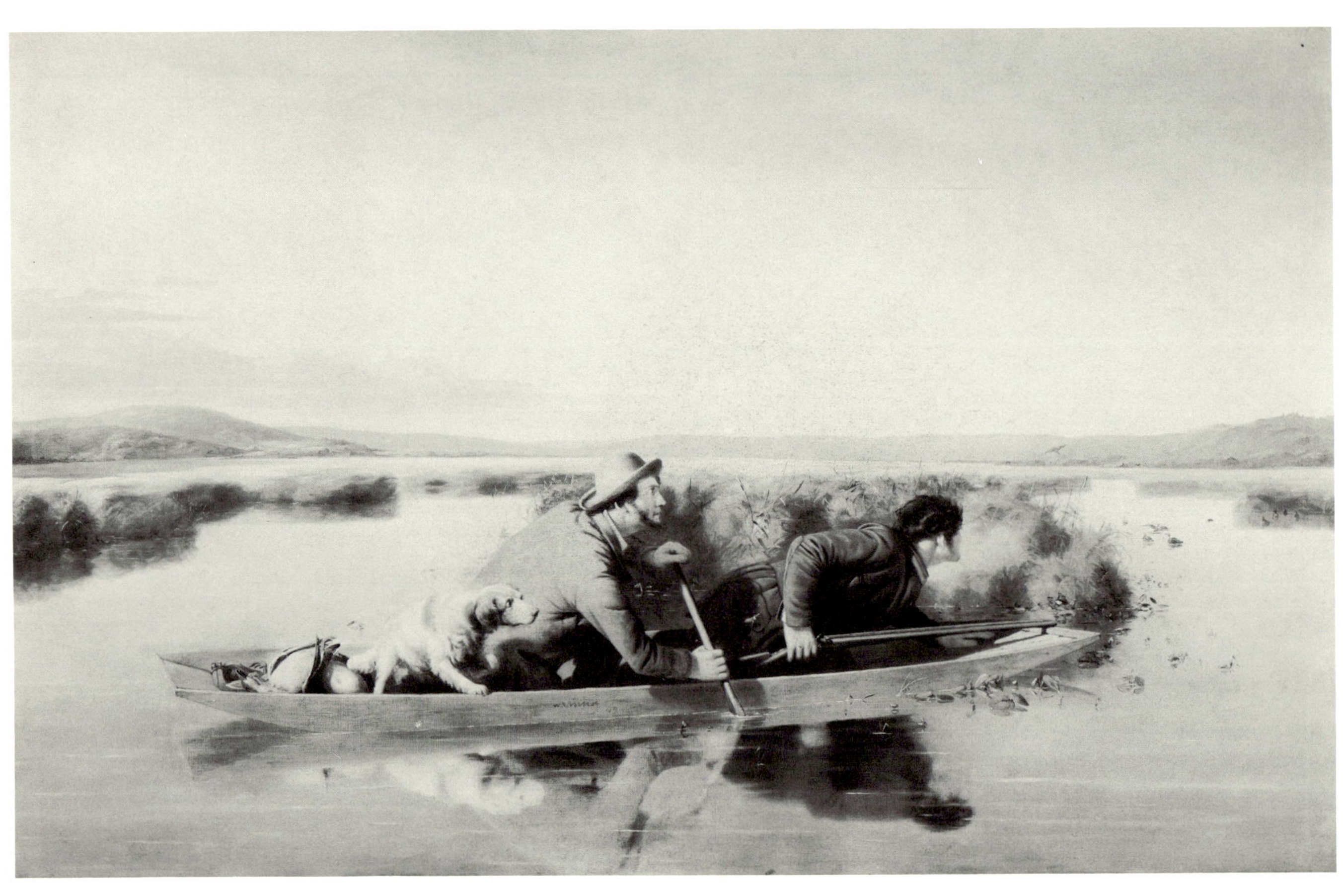

28. WILLIAM TYLEE RANNEY (1813–1857). *Duck Hunters on the Hoboken Marshes*, 1849. 26 x 40 in. 48.470

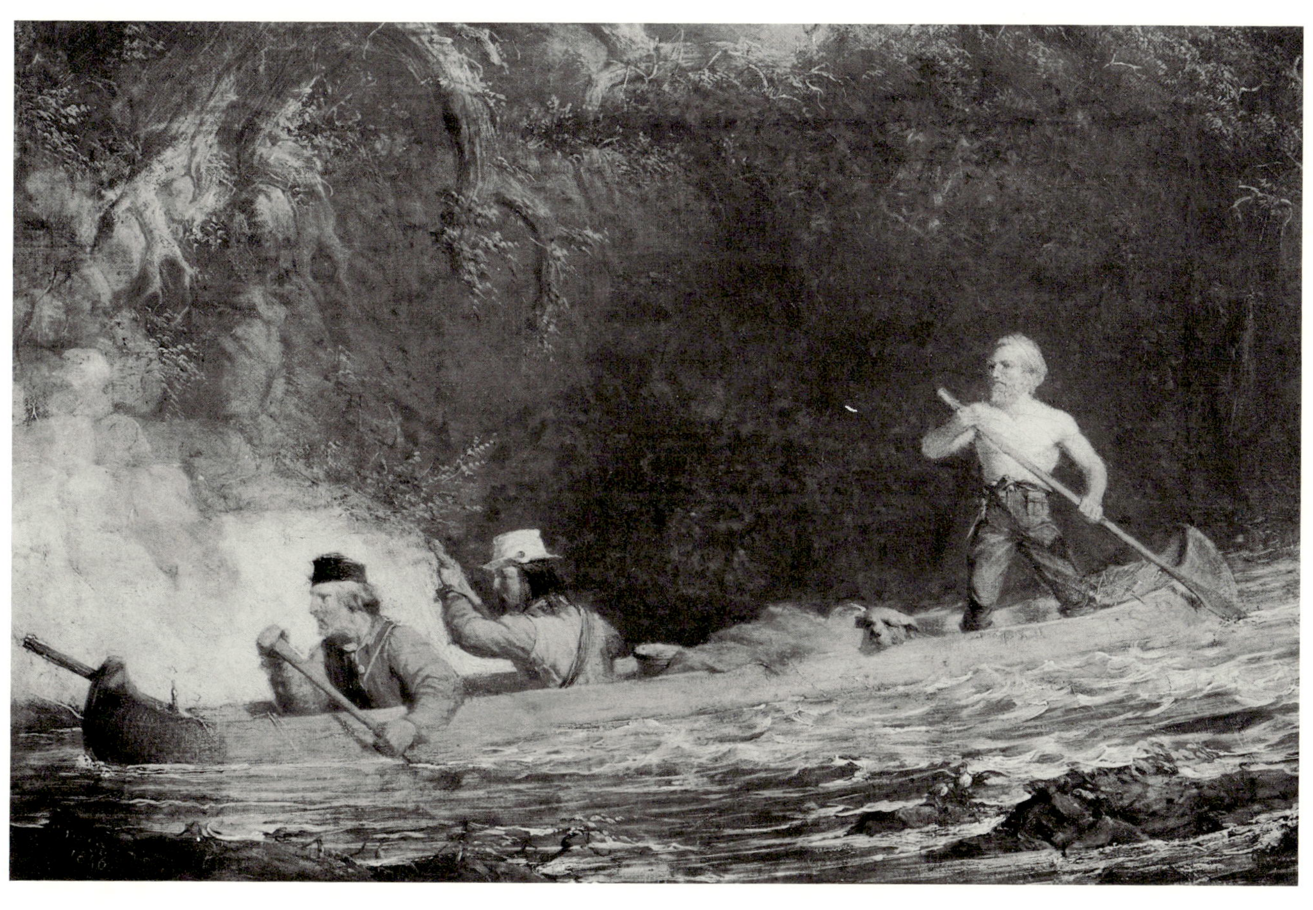

29. CHARLES DEAS (1818–1867). *The Voyageurs*, 1846. 13 x 20½ in. 46.855

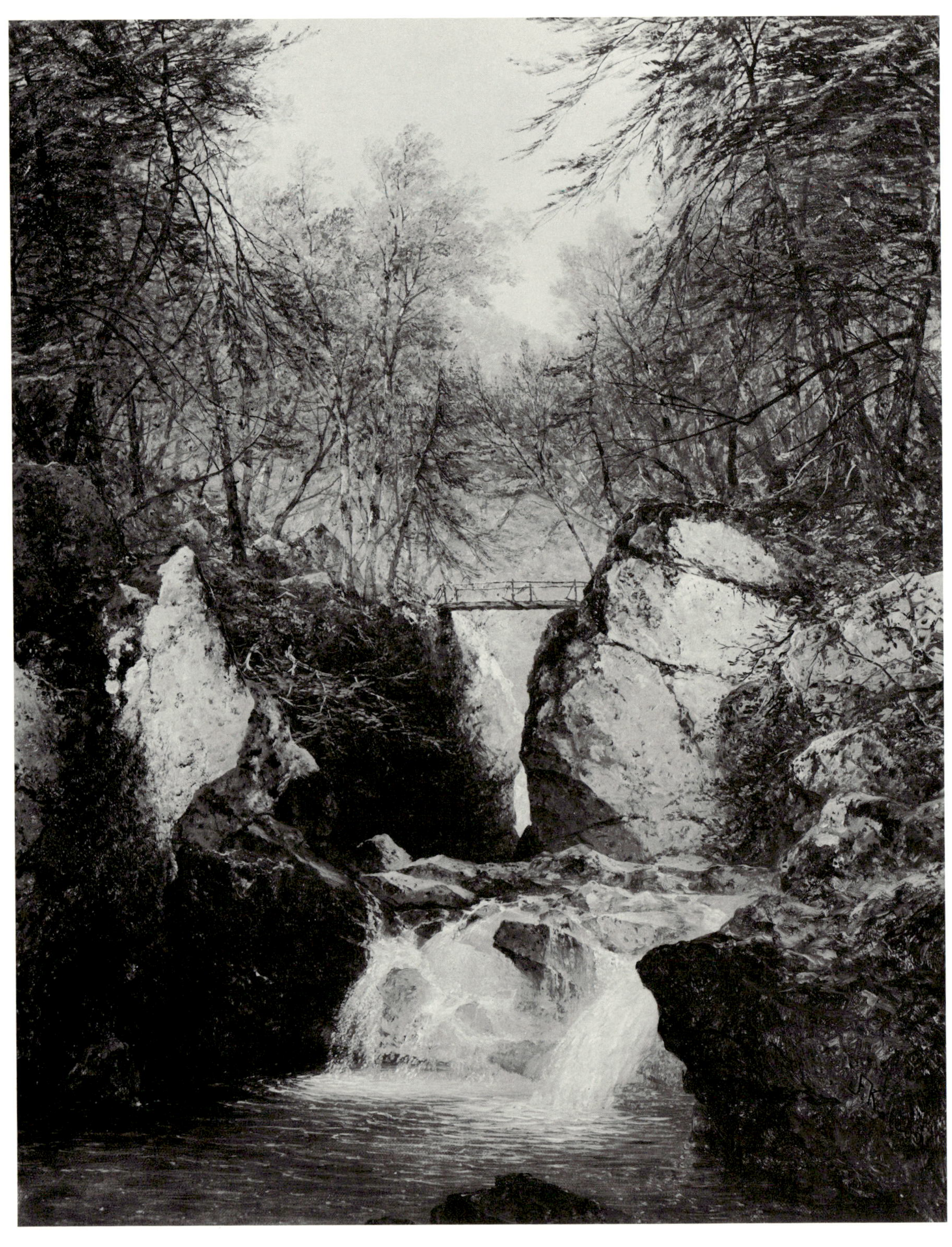

30. JOHN FREDERICK KENSETT (1816–1872).
Bash-Bish Falls, South Egremont, Massachusetts, 1855. 29½ x 24 in. 48.437

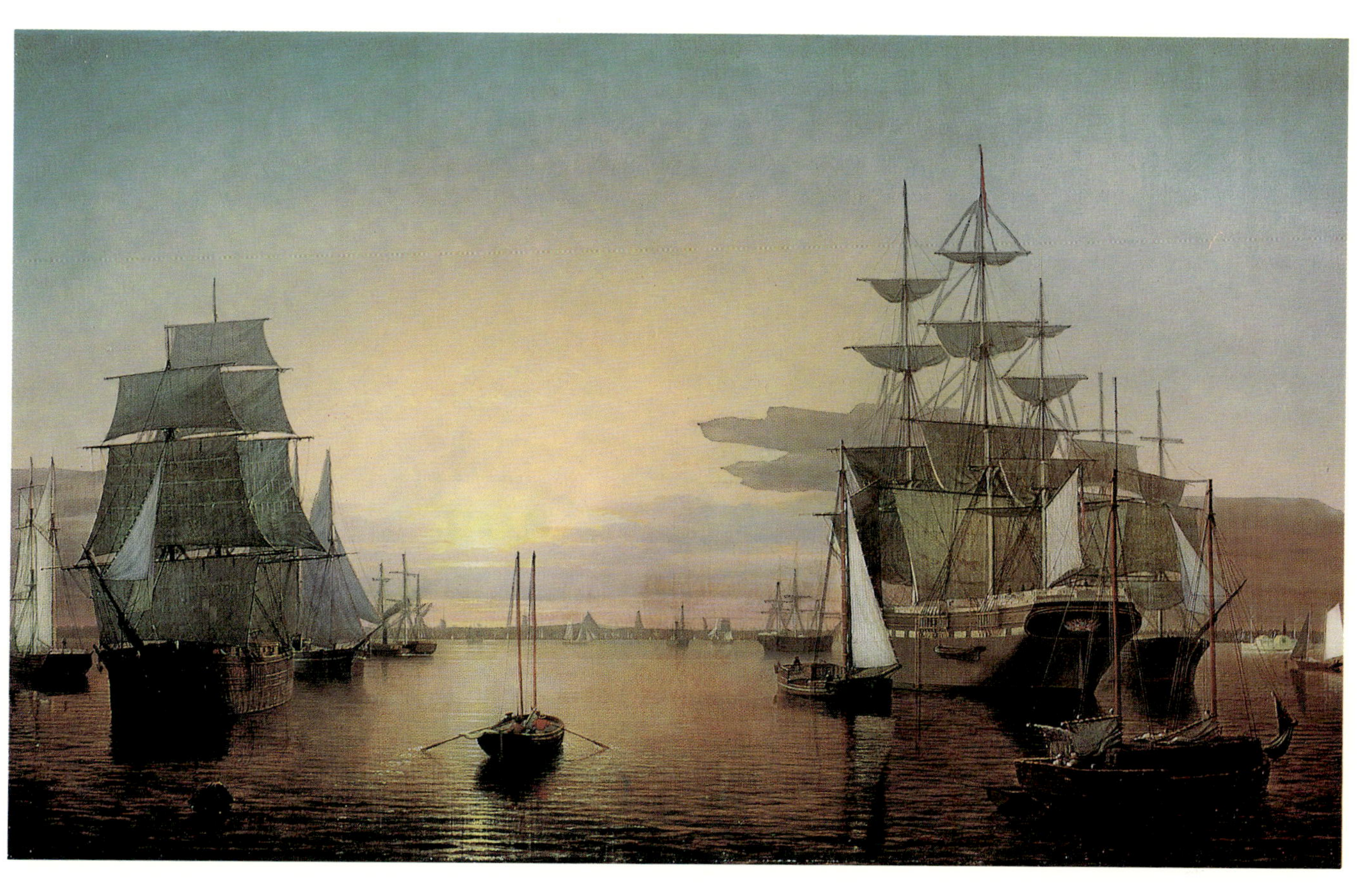

31. Fitz Hugh Lane (1804–1865).
Boston Harbor, about 1850–1855. 26¼ x 32 in. 66.339

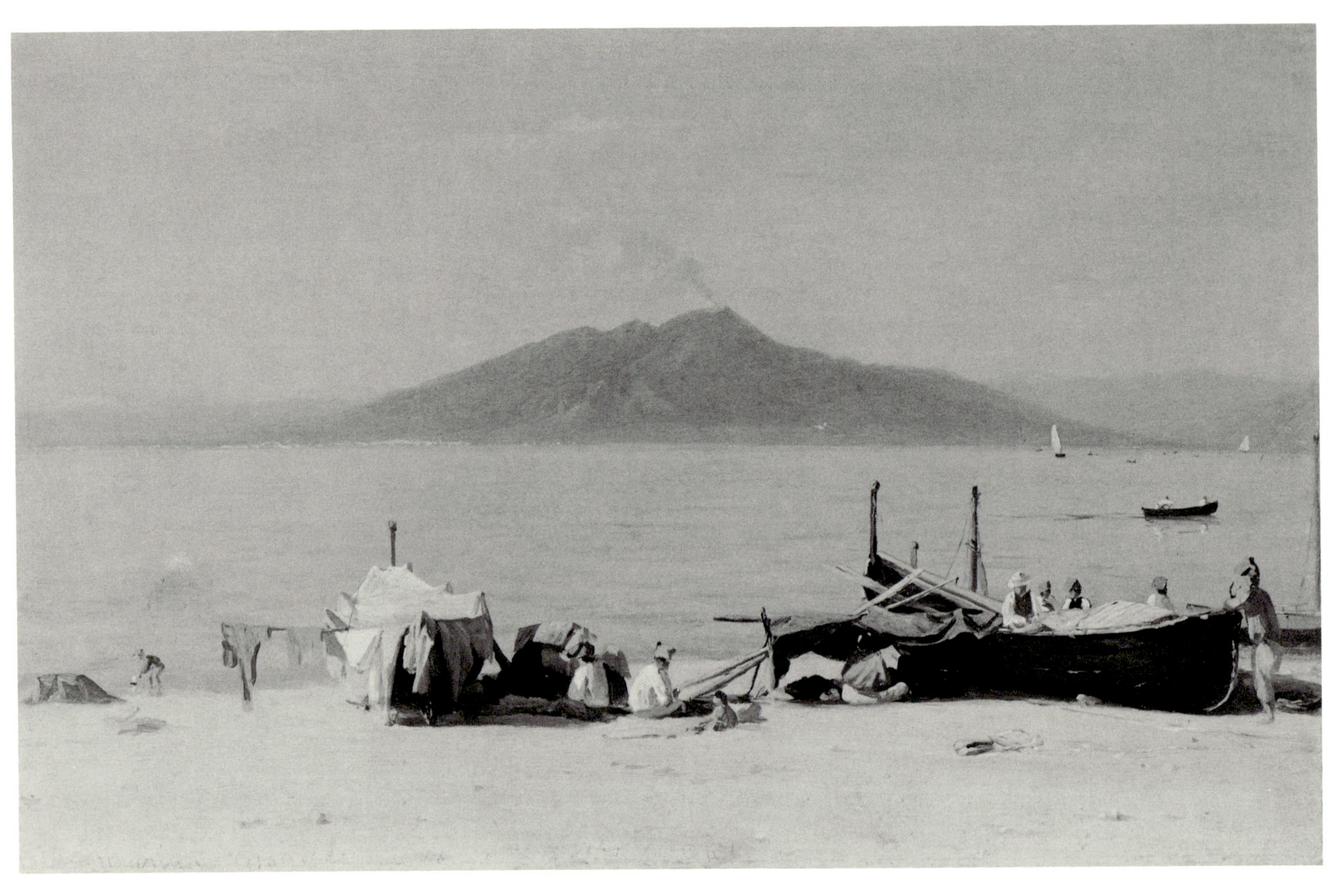

32. Sanford Robinson Gifford (1823–1880). *Marina Grande near Sorrento*, 1857. 9 x 14 in. 64.428

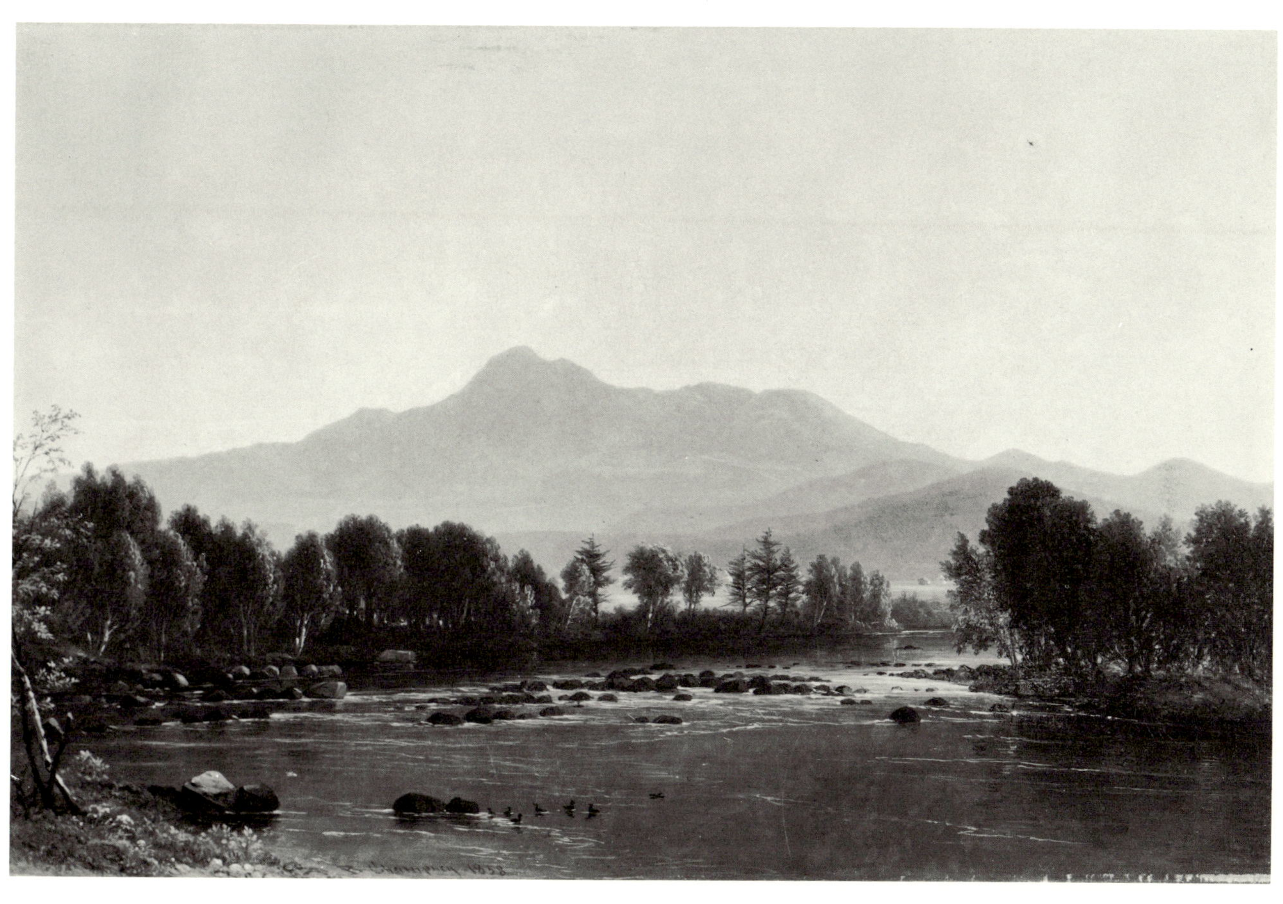

33. BENJAMIN CHAMPNEY (1817–1907). *Mount Chocorua, New Hampshire*, 1858. 12 x 18 in. 64.423

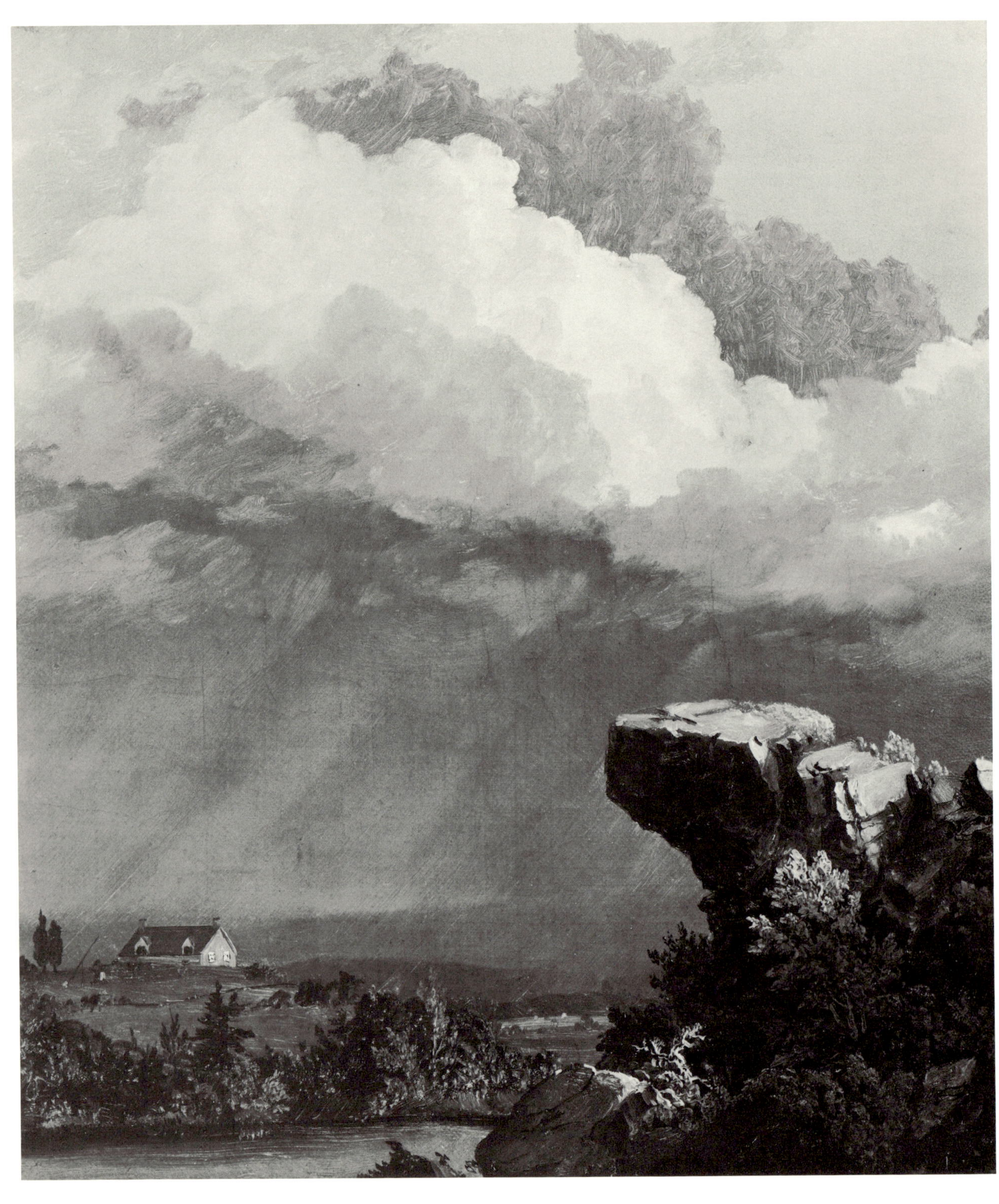

34. FREDERIC EDWIN CHURCH (1826–1900). *The Harp of the Winds*, about 1850. 14 x 12 in. 48.415

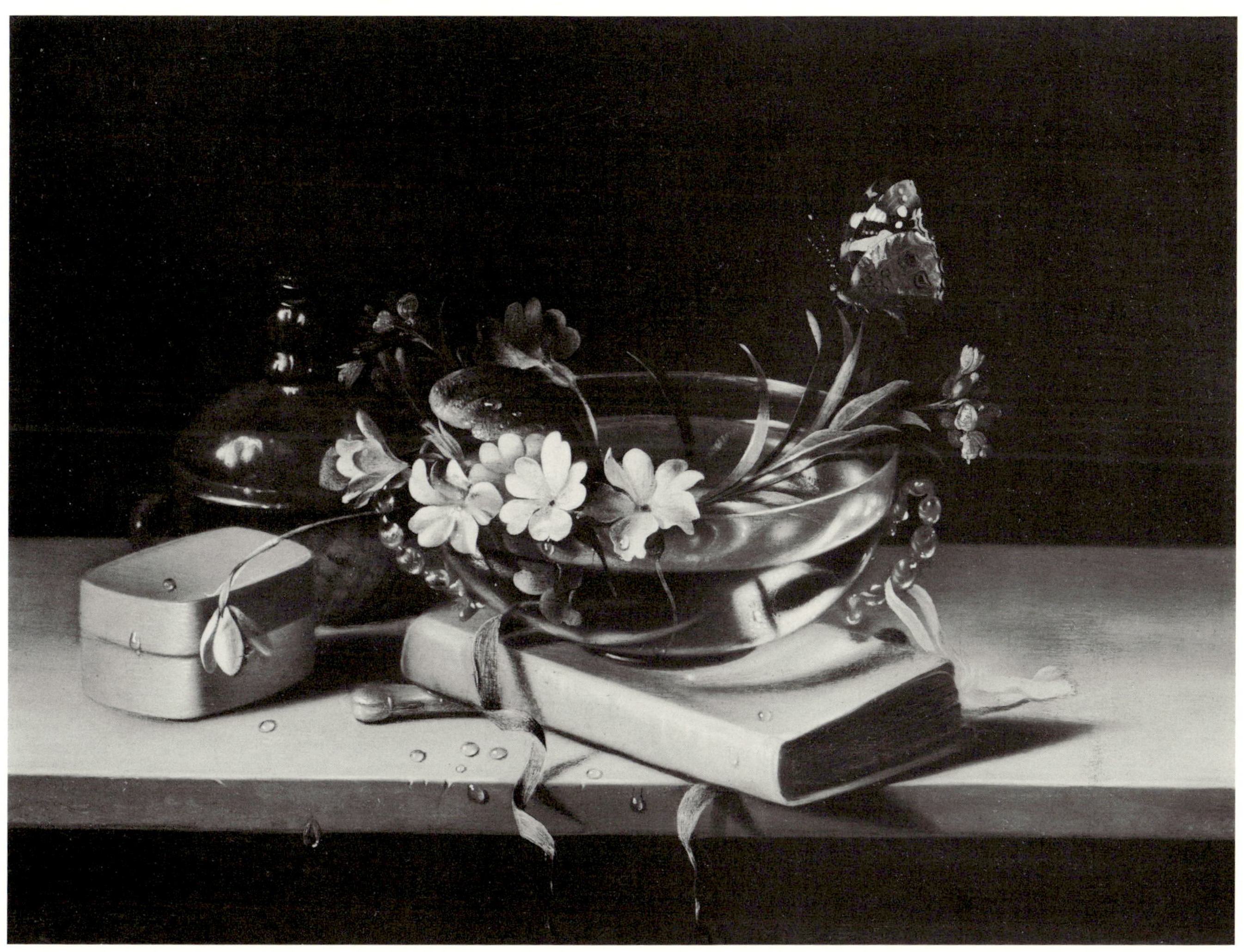

35. ANONYMOUS. *Flowers, Butterfly, and Book*, before 1850. 10½ x 14¼ in. 47.1252

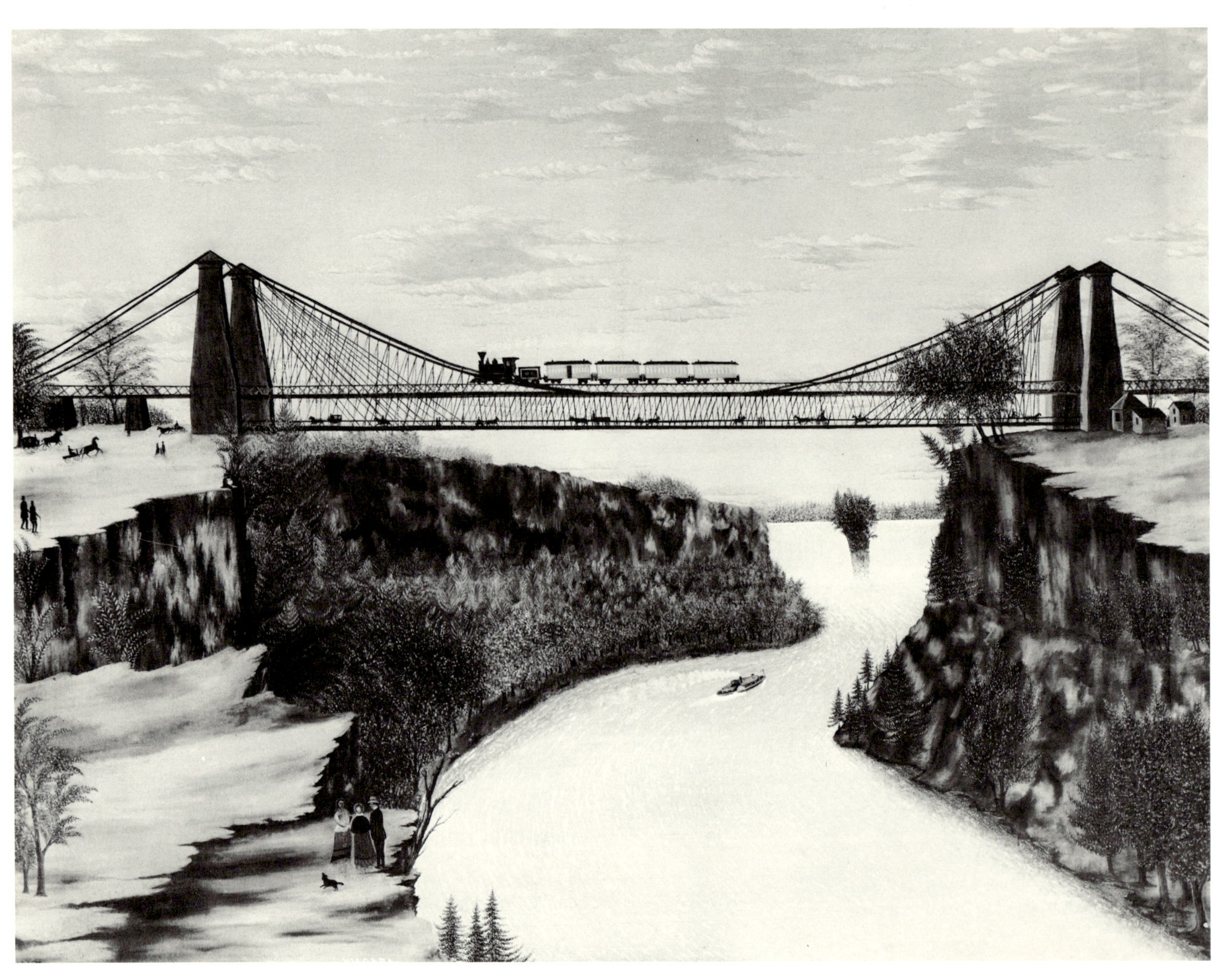

36. ANONYMOUS. *The Railroad Suspension Bridge near Niagara Falls*, after 1855. 30¼ x 39 in. 62.259

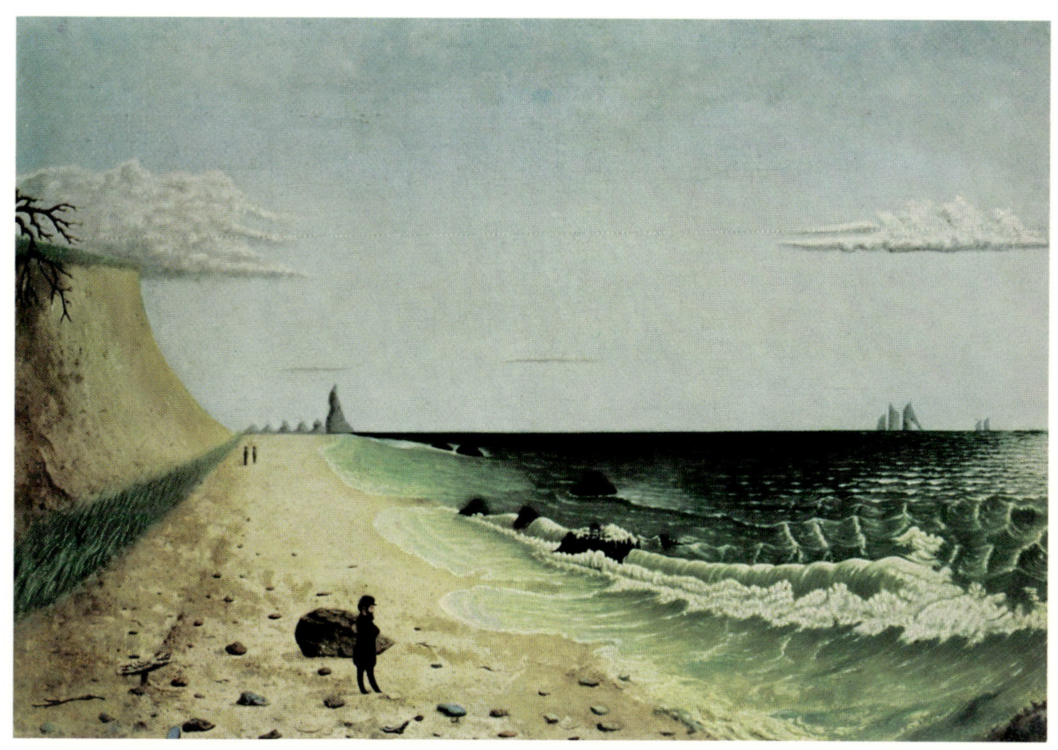

37. ANONYMOUS. *Meditation by the Sea*, about 1850–1860. 13½ x 19½ in. 45.892

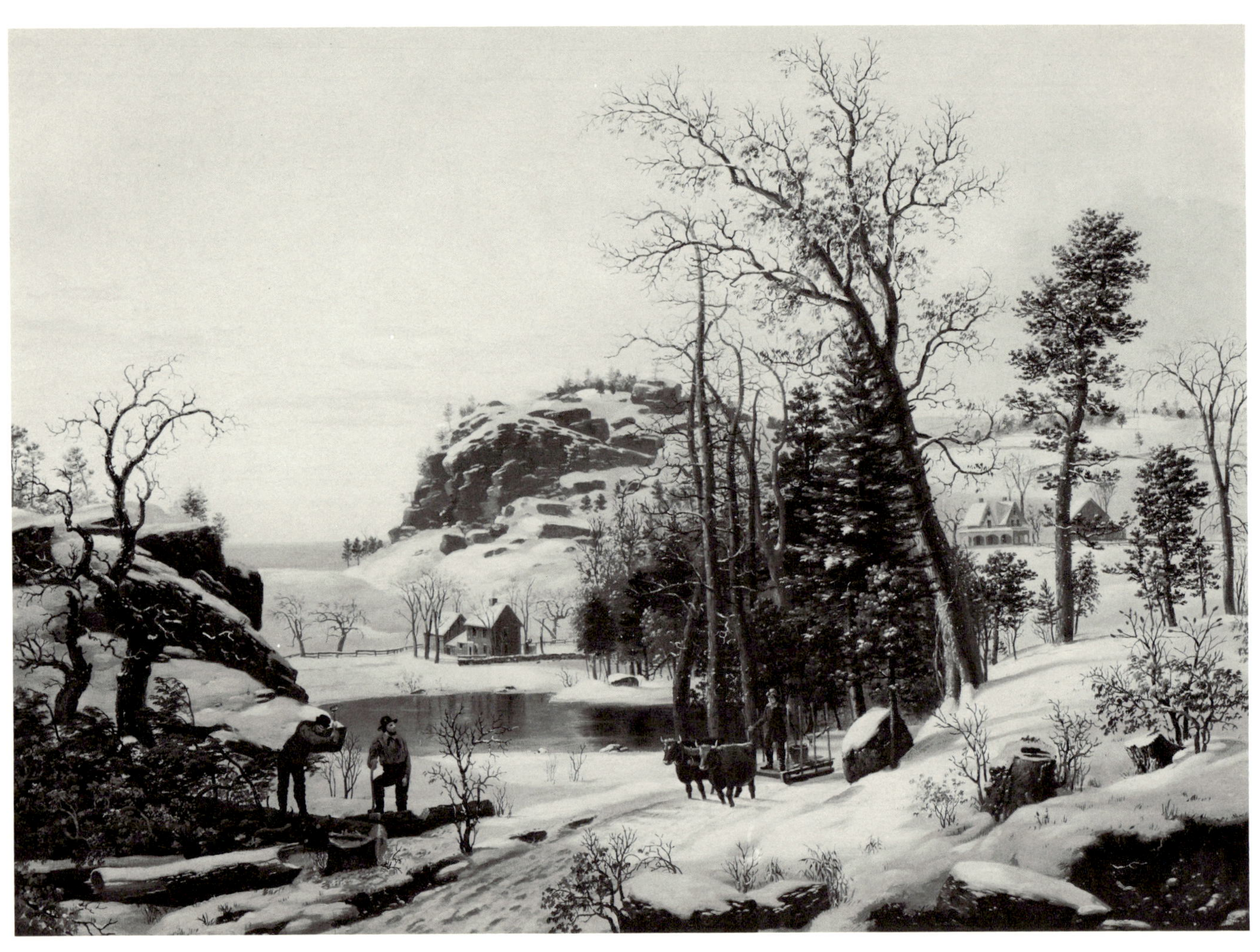

38. Anonymous. *Woodcutting in Winter*, about 1850–1860. 26¼ x 36¼ in. 48.409

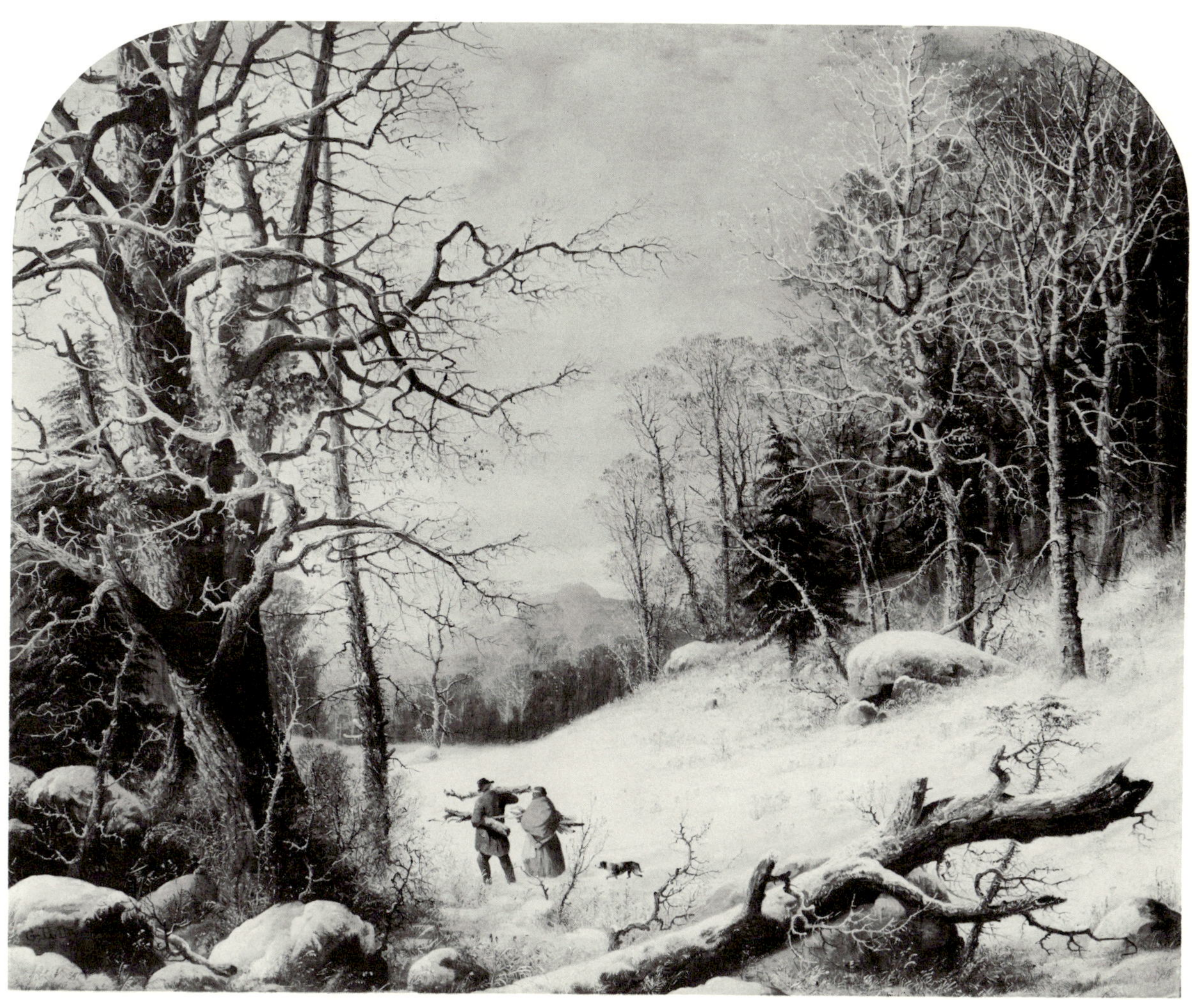

39. George Henry Durrie (1820–1863). *Winter Landscape: Gathering Wood*, 1859. 28 x 34¼ in. 46.853

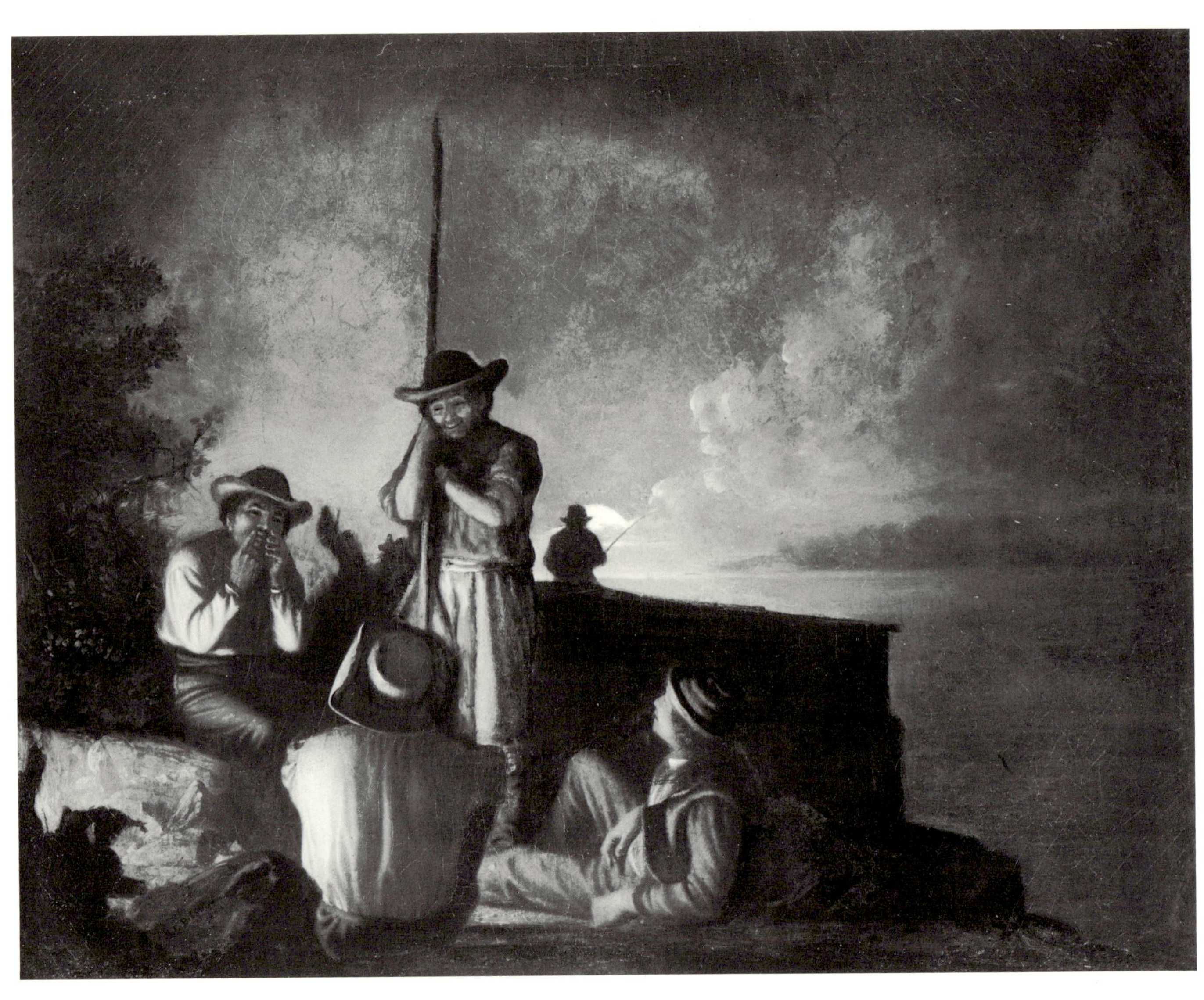

40. GEORGE CALEB BINGHAM (1811–1879).
Wood-Boatmen on a River, 1854. 29 x 36 in. 46.848

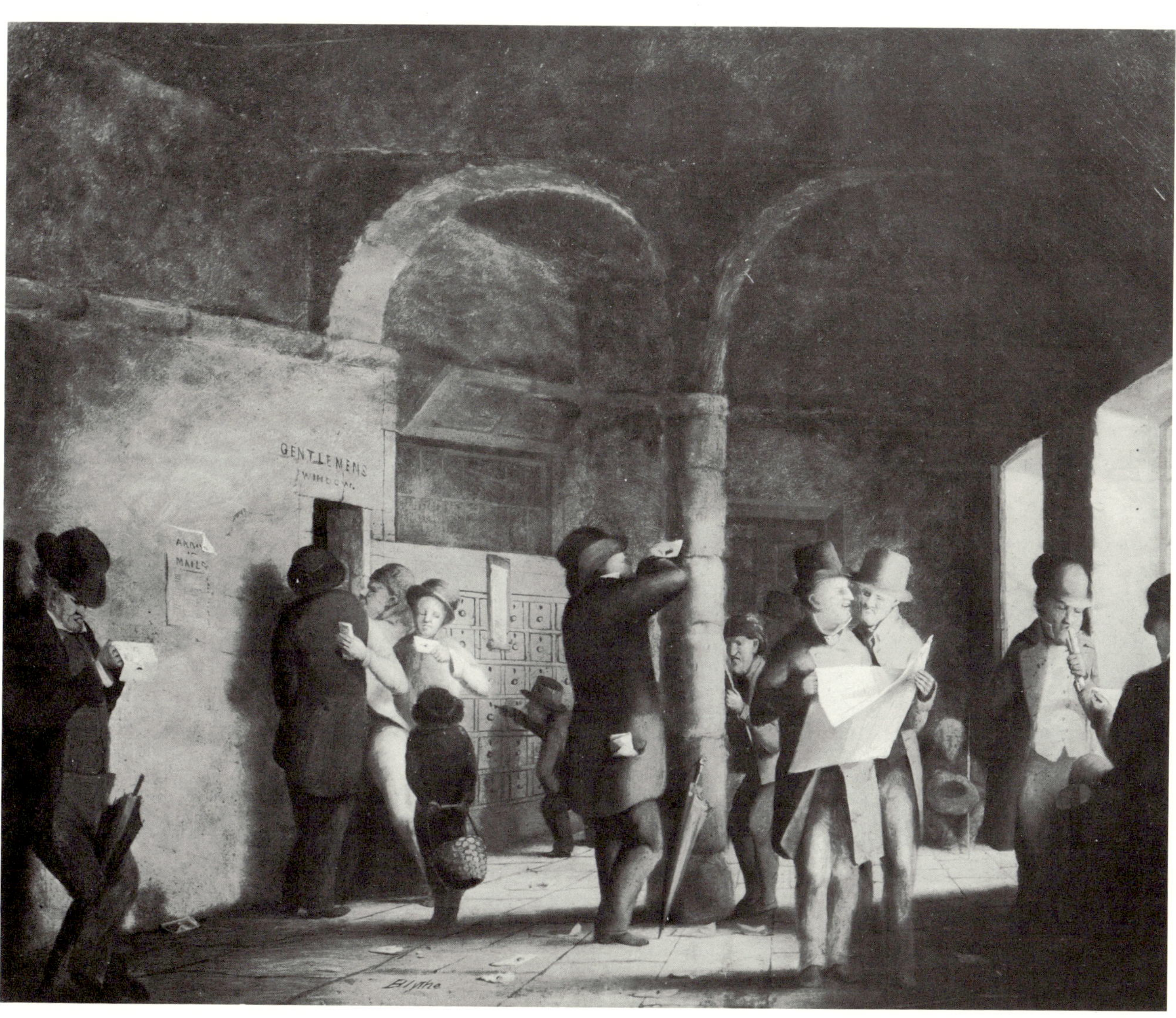

41. DAVID GILMOUR BLYTHE (1815–1865).
In the Pittsburgh Post Office, about 1856–1861. 25 x 30 in. 46.849

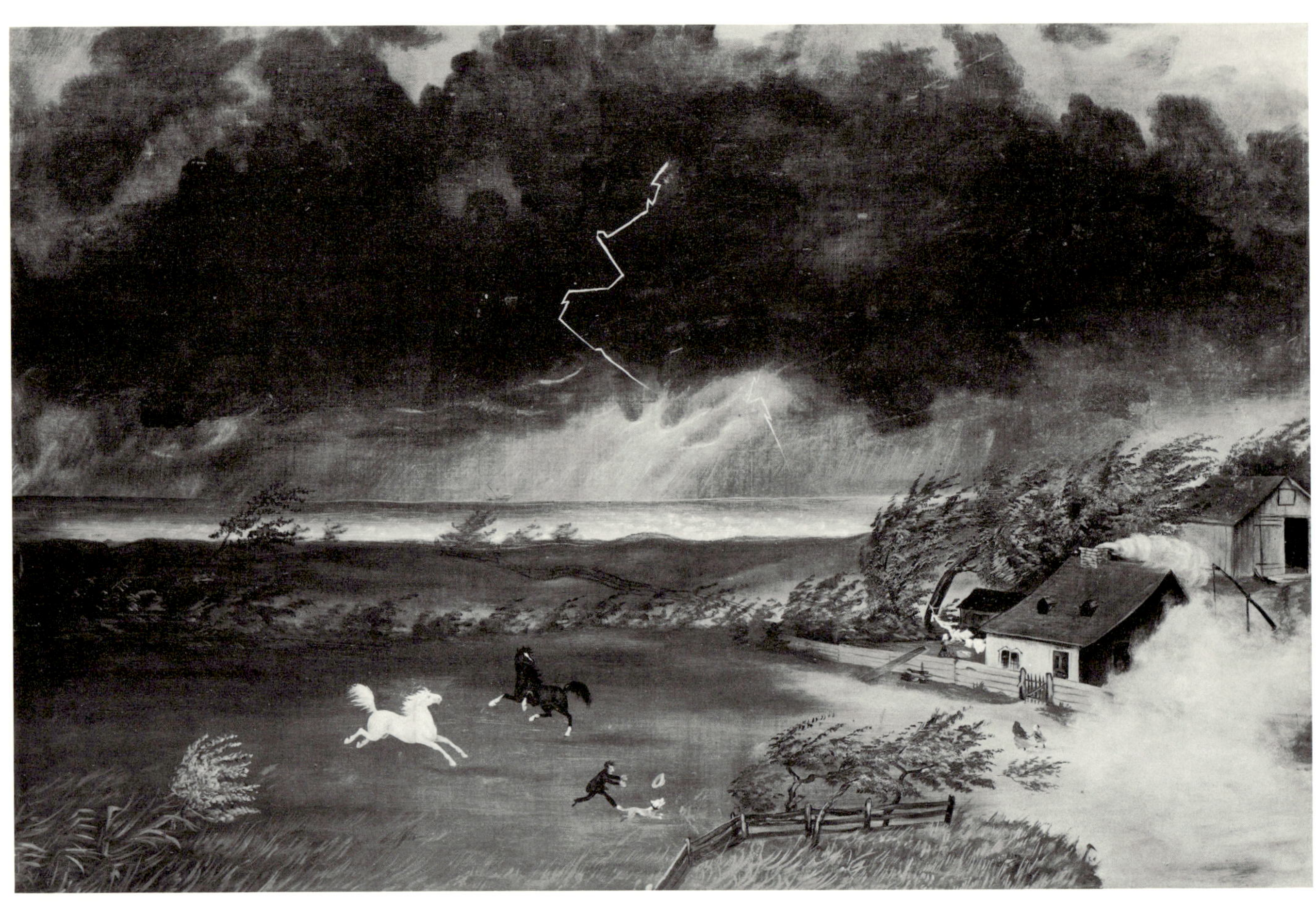

42. ANONYMOUS. *Running before the Storm*, after 1877. 24 x 36¼ in. 46.851

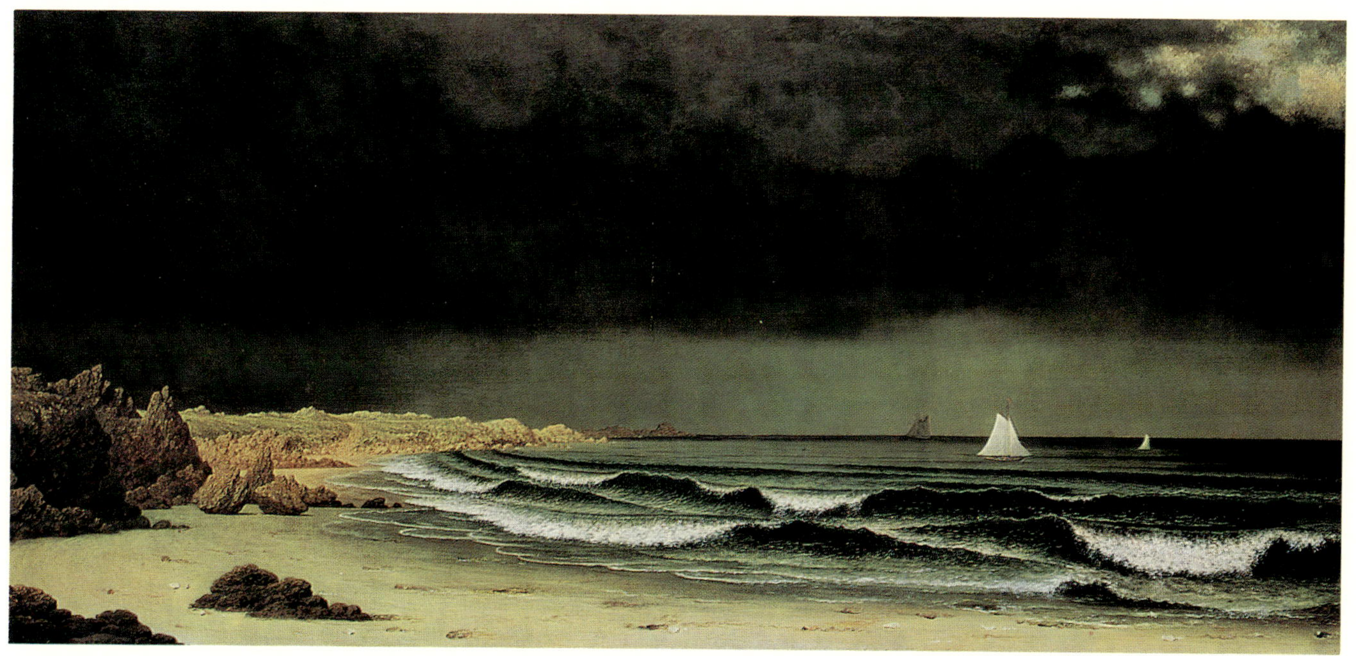

43. Martin Johnson Heade (1819–1904). *Approaching Storm: Beach near Newport*, 1860's. 28 x 58¼ in. 45.889

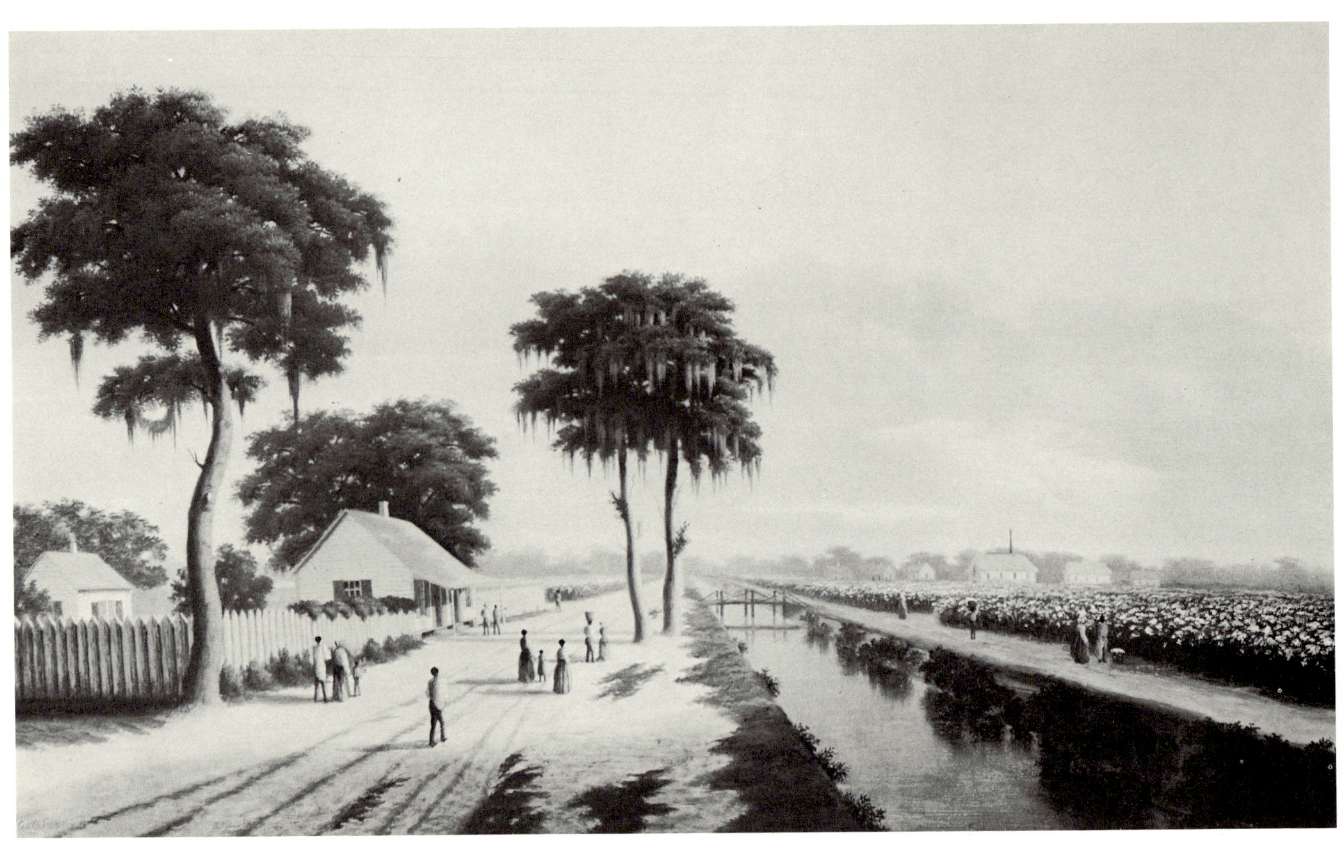

44. C. Giroux. *Cotton Plantation*, 1850–1865. 22 x 36 in. 47.1144

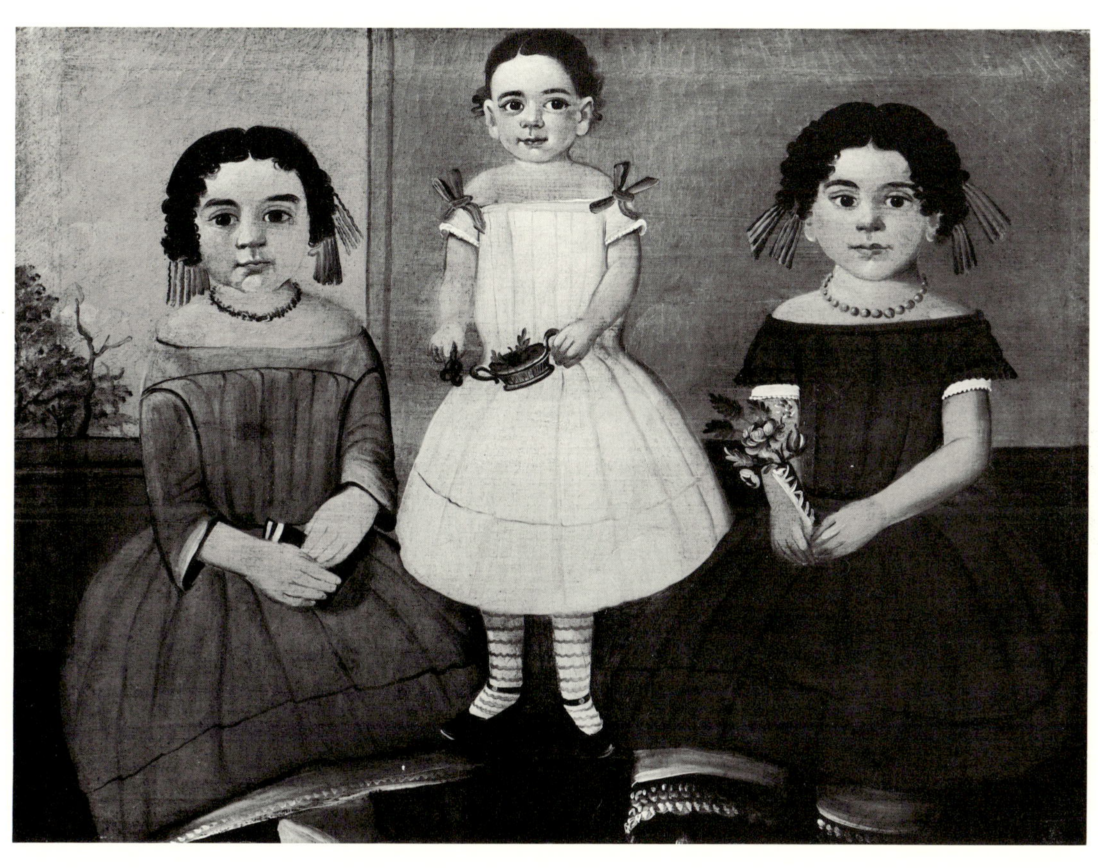

45. WILLIAM MATTHEW PRIOR (1806–1873).
Three Sisters of the Coplan Family, 1854. 26¾ x 36¼ in. 48.467

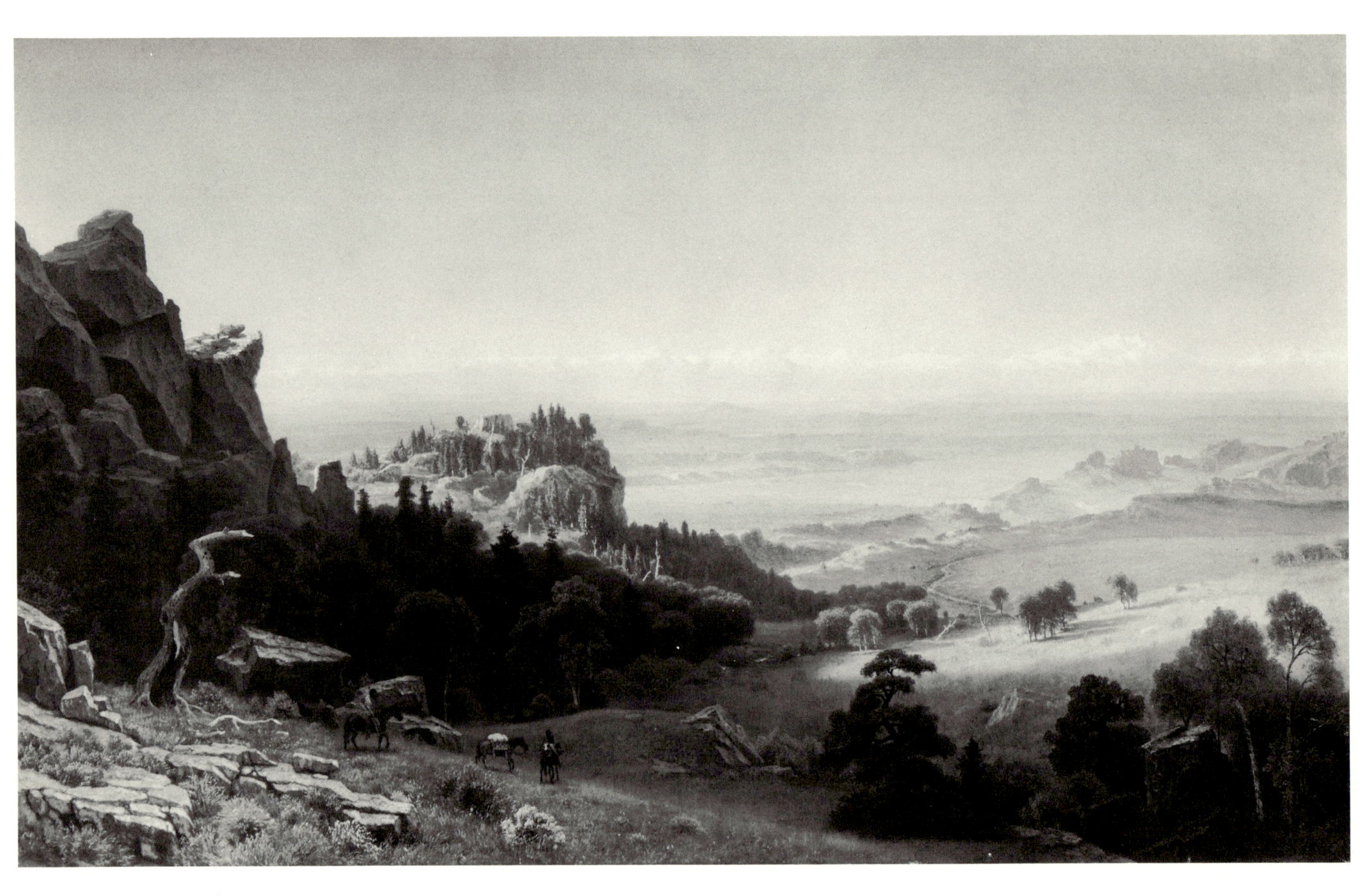

46. Albert Bierstadt (1830–1902).
View from the Wind River Mountains, Wyoming, 1860. 30¼ x 48¼ in. 47.1202

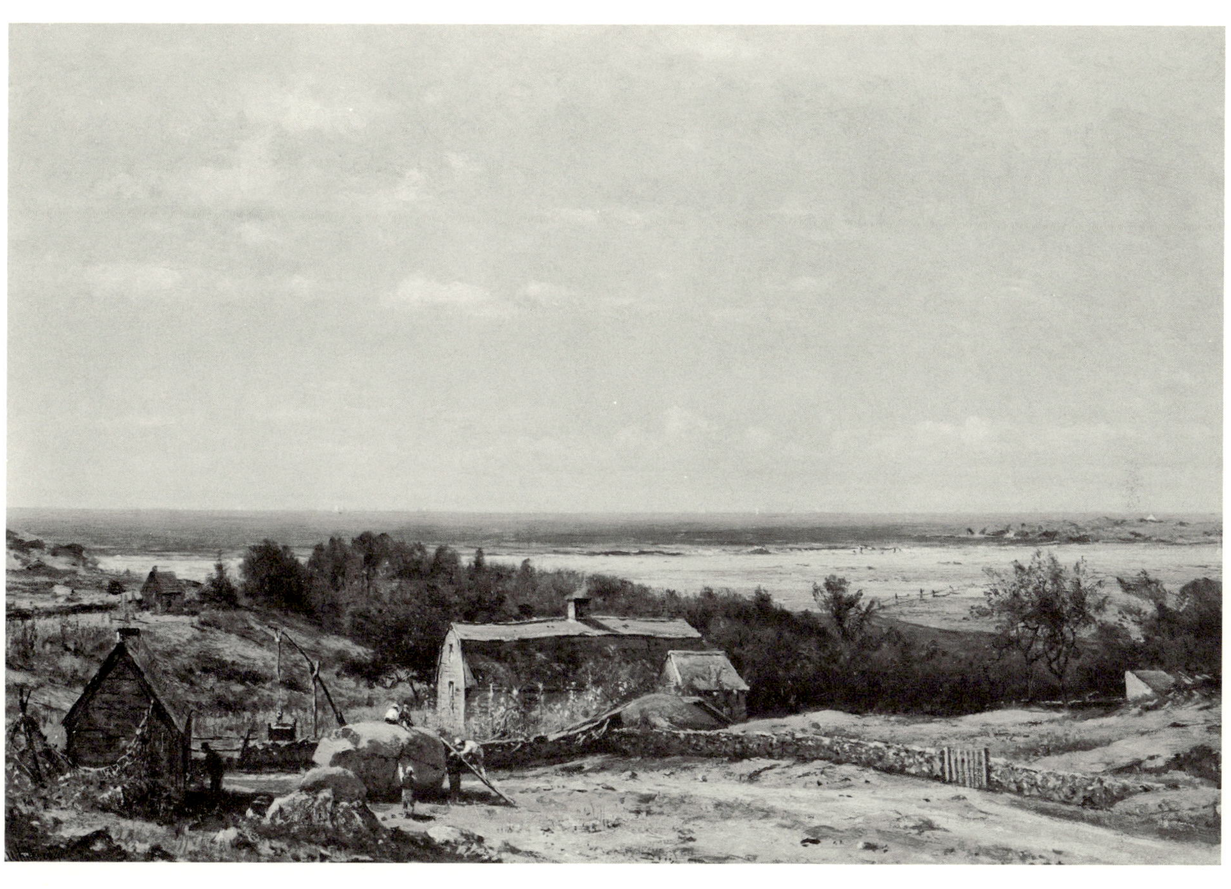

47. Thomas Worthington Whittredge (1820–1910).
Old Homestead by the Sea, 1883. 22 x 32 in. 48.492

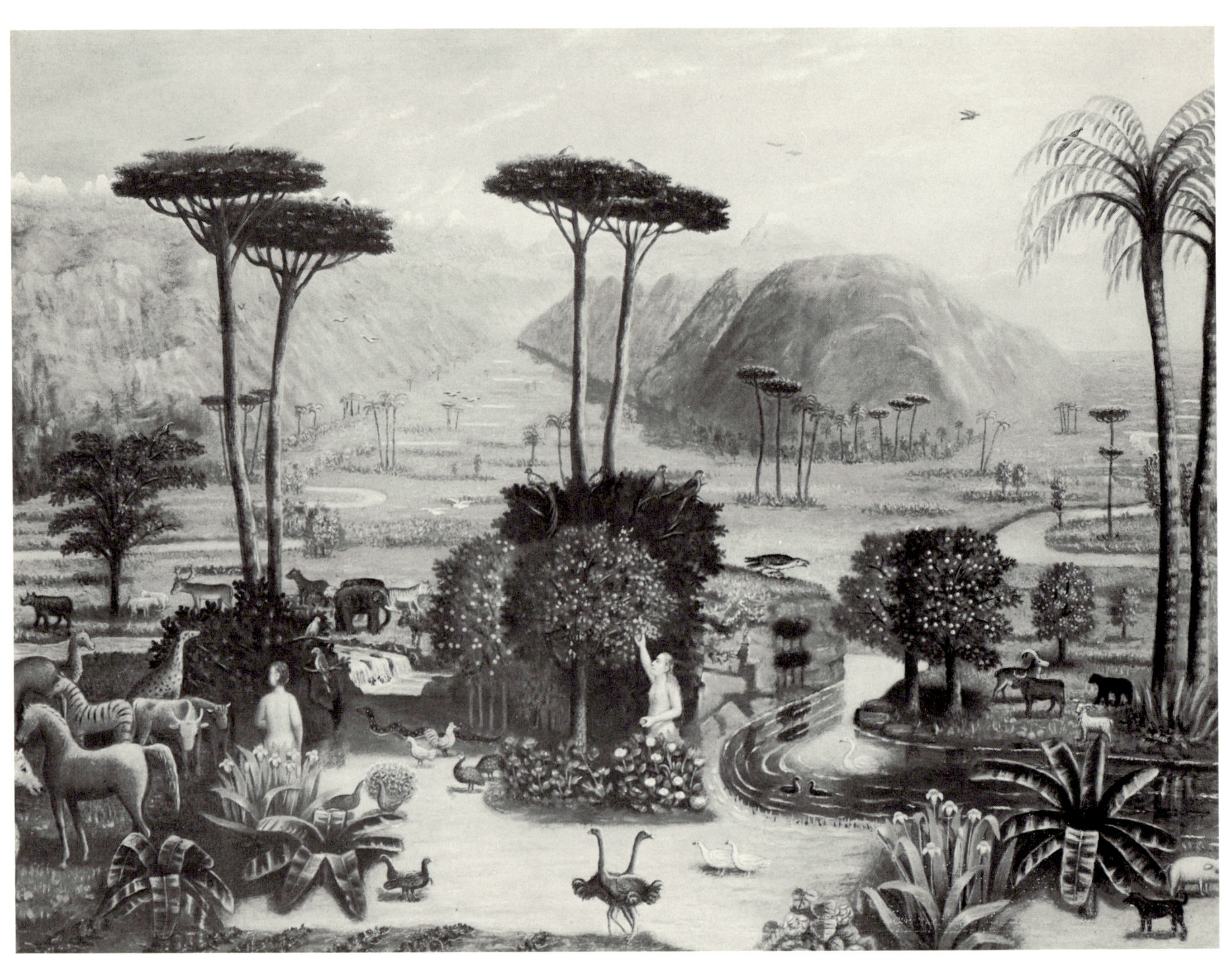

48. ERASTUS SALISBURY FIELD (1805–1900).
The Garden of Eden, about 1860–1870. 34³/₄ x 46 in. 48.1027

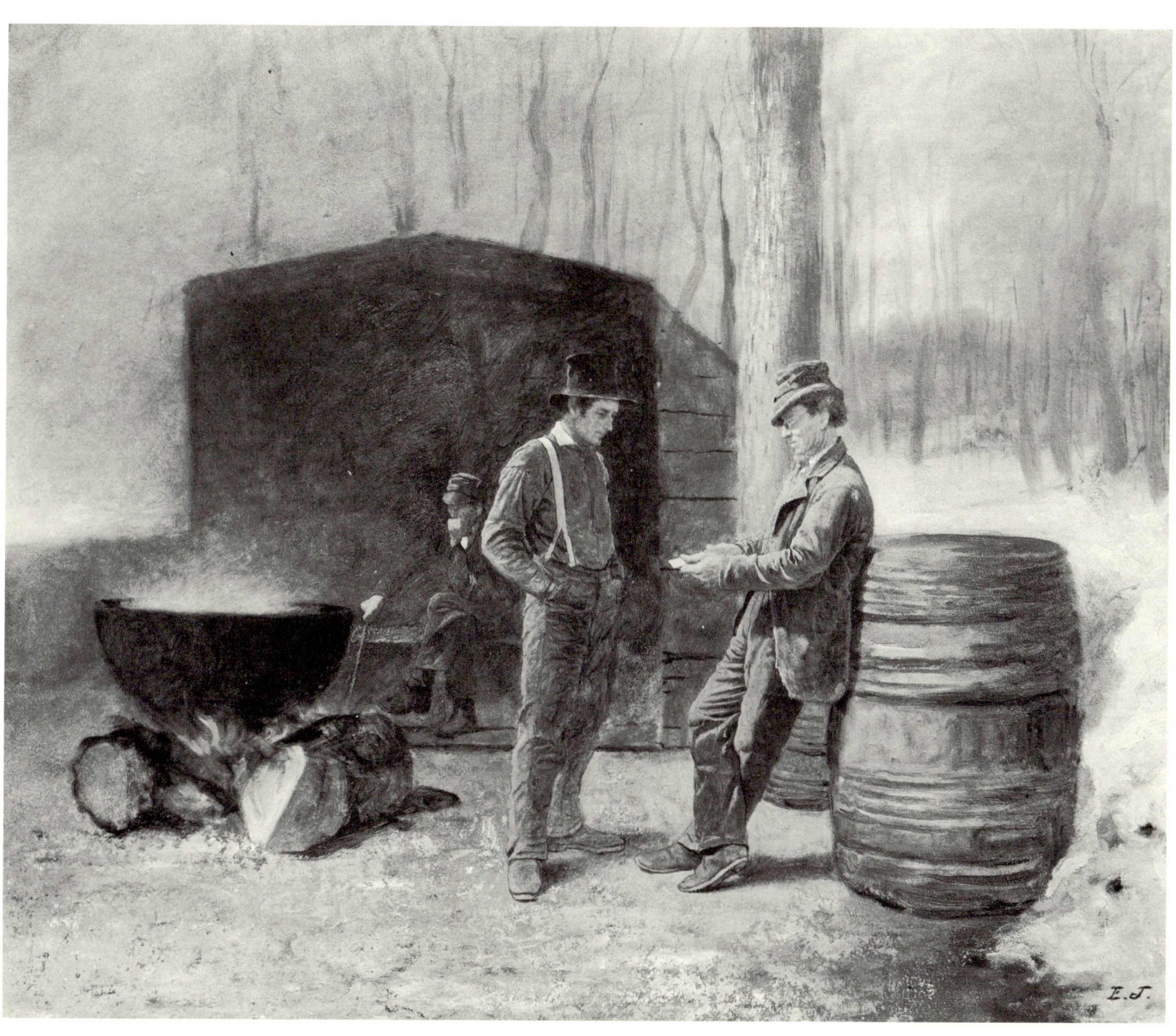

49. JONATHAN EASTMAN JOHNSON (1824–1906).
Measurement and Contemplation, early 1860's. 20 x 24 in. 48.435

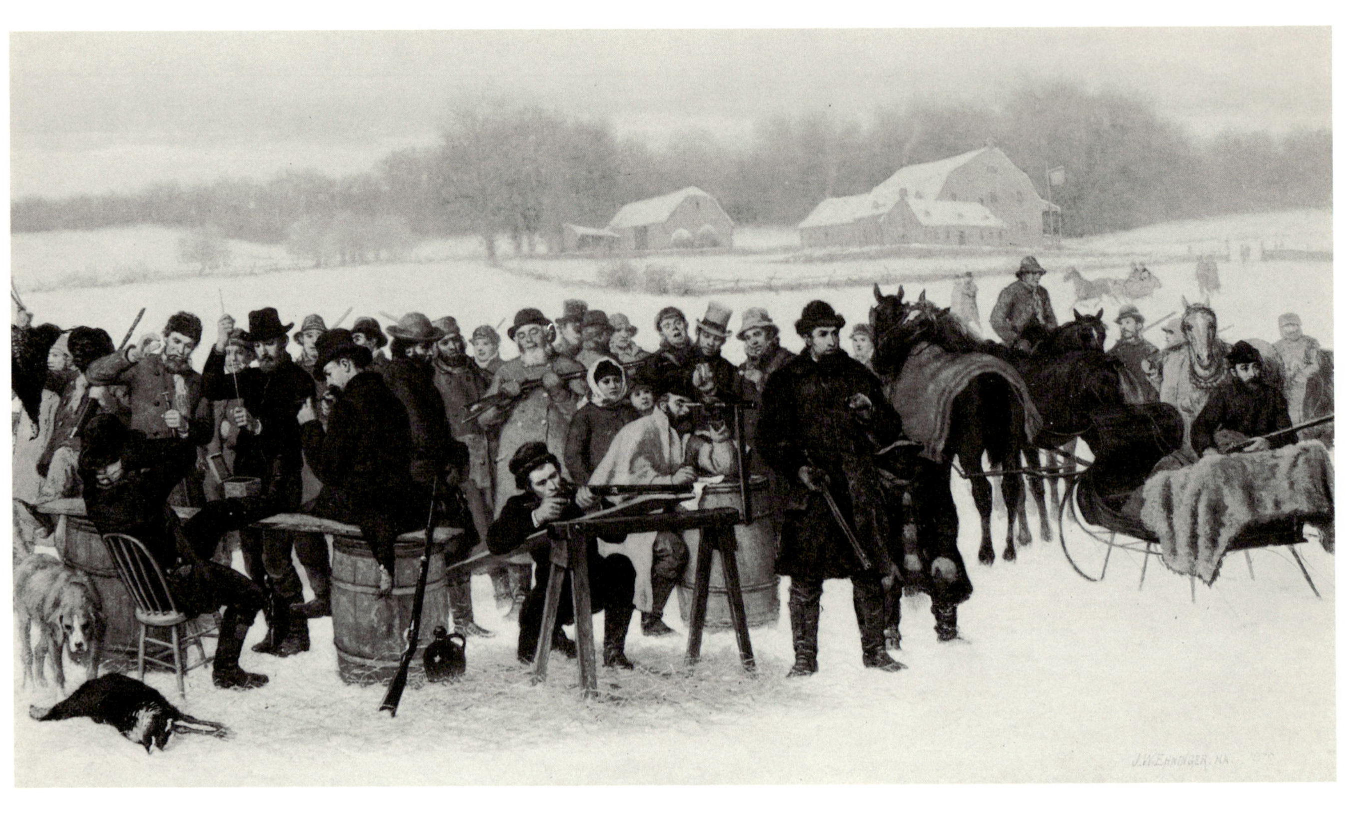

50. John Whetten Ehninger (1827–1889). *Turkey Shoot*, 1879. 25 x 43½ in. 46.854

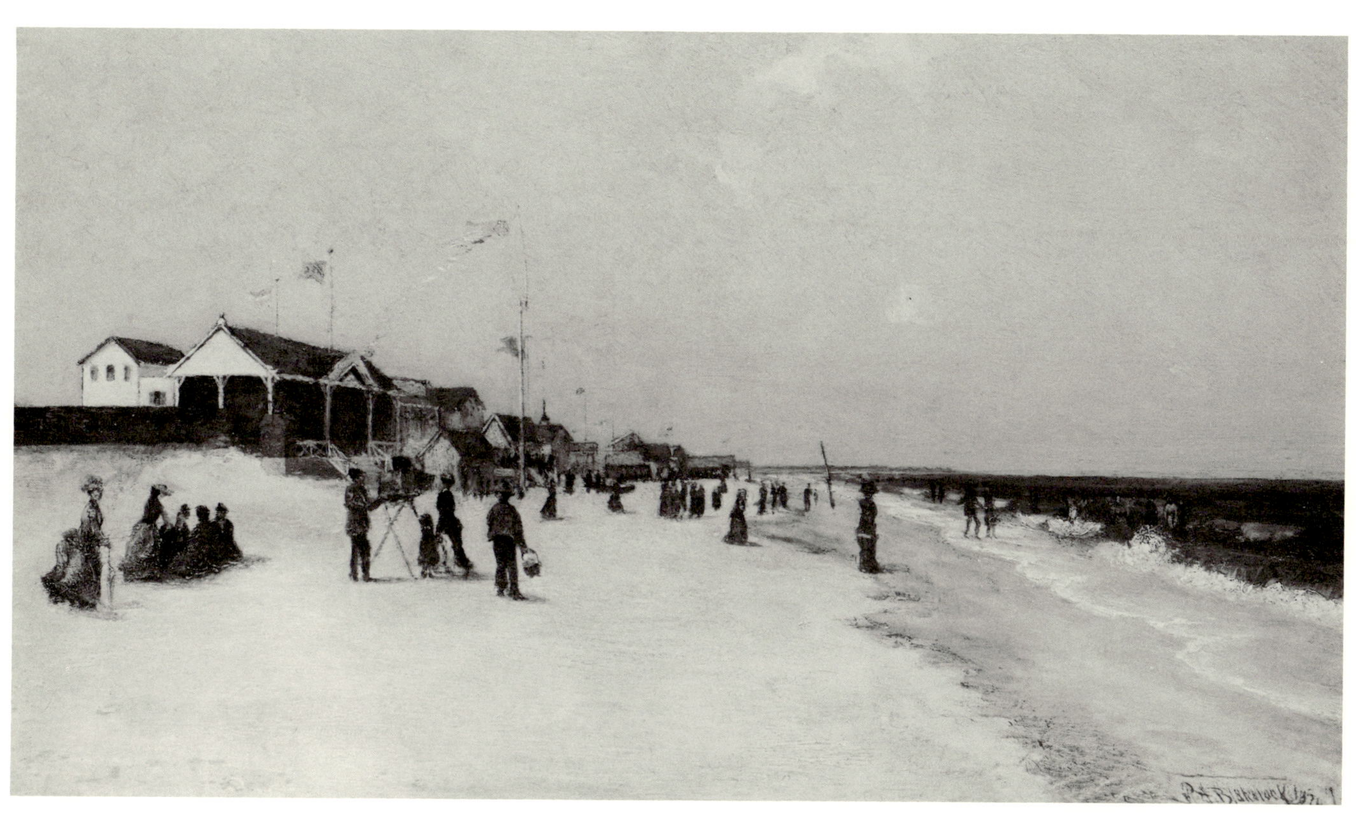

51. RALPH ALBERT BLAKELOCK (1847–1919).
Rockaway Beach, Long Island, New York, about 1869–1870. 11¾ x 20 in. 62.262

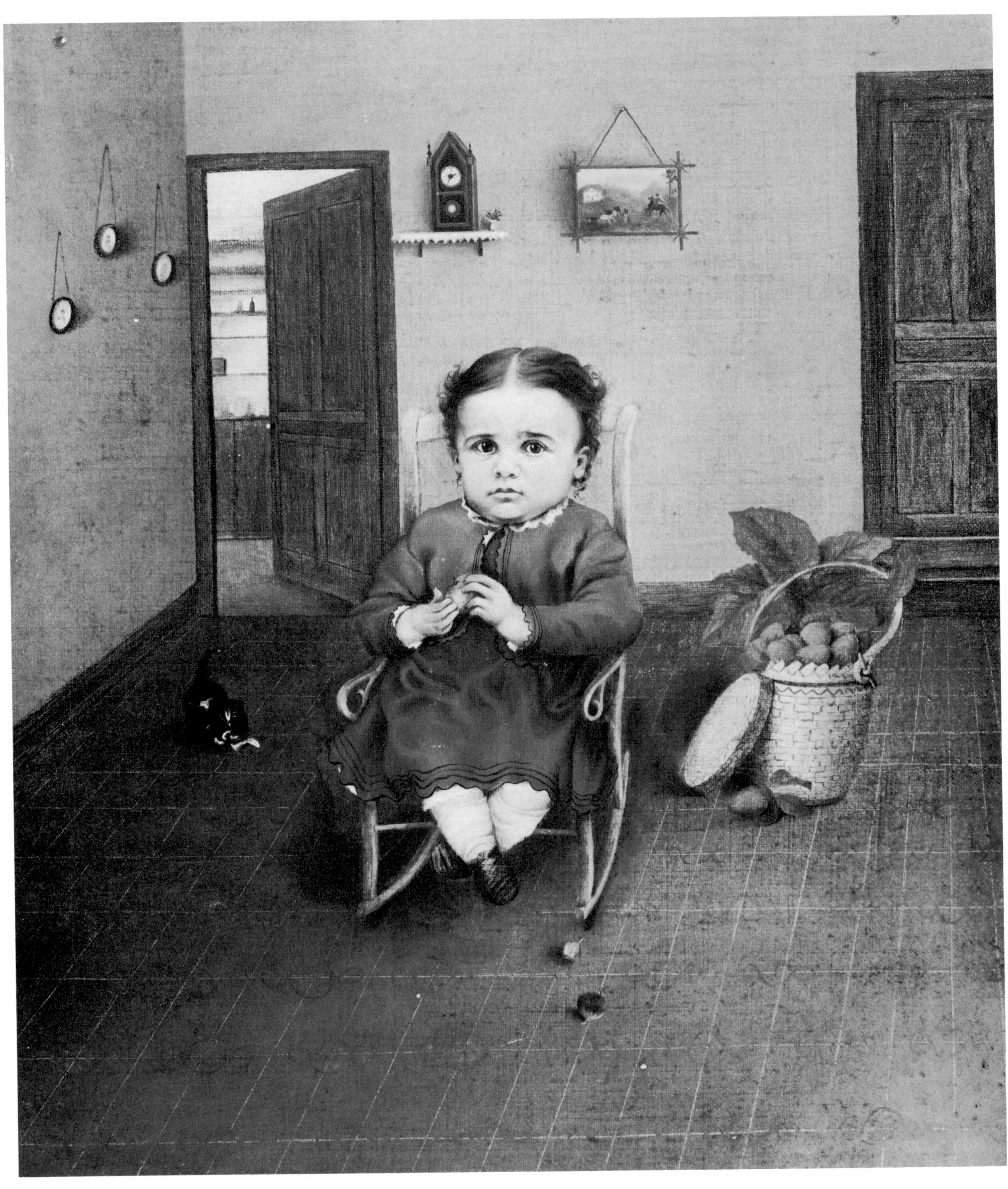

52. E. L. George. *Child in a Rocking Chair*, 1870. 15 x 13 in. 62.272

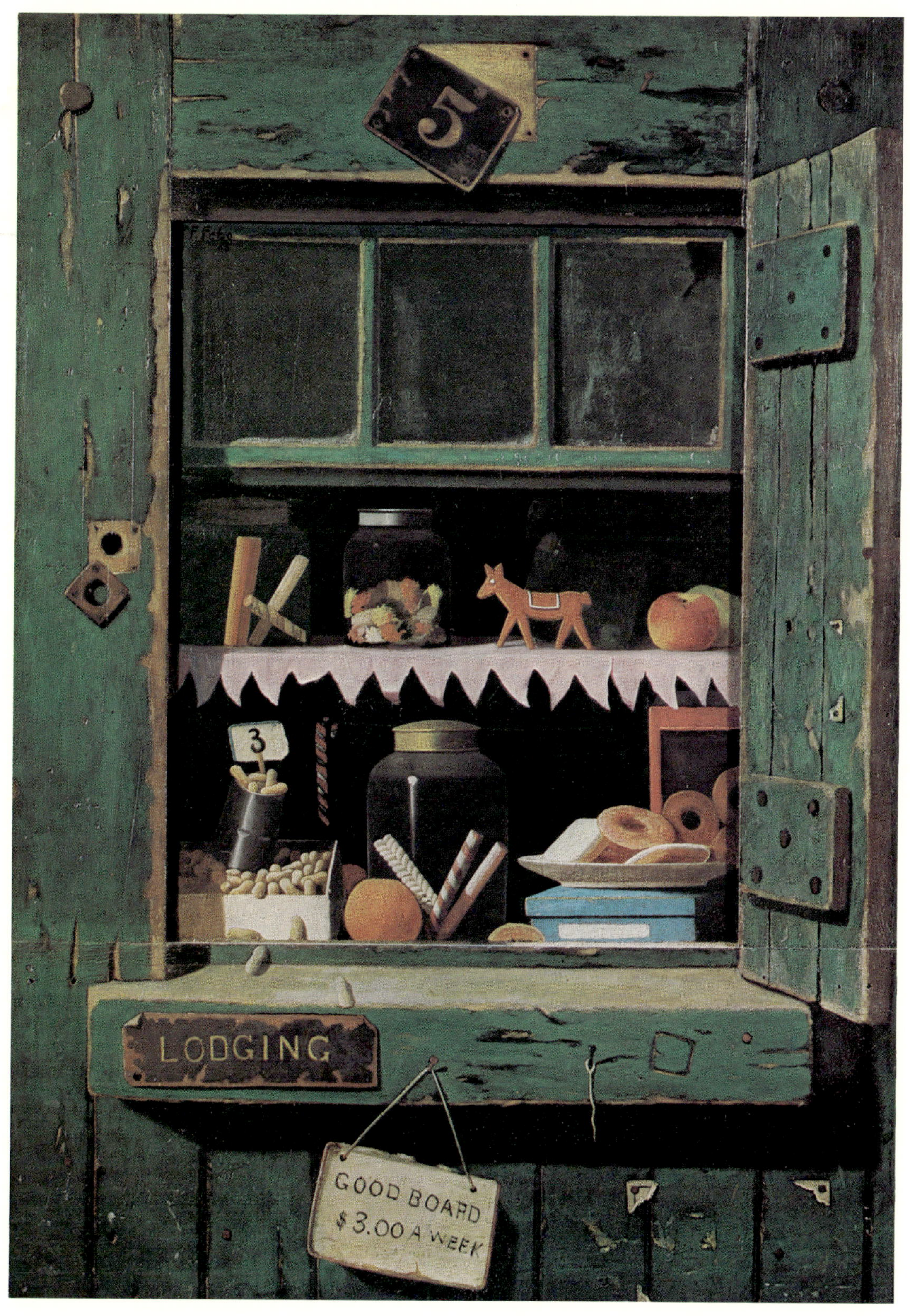

53. JOHN FREDERICK PETO (1854–1907). *The Poor Man's Store*, 1885. 36 x 25½ in. 62.278